# How To Survive Your First 90 Days At A New Company

# How To Survive Your First 90 Days At A New Company

By Paul Kaponya

THE CAREER PRESS
62 BEVERLY RD., PO BOX 34
HAWTHORNE, NJ 07507
TOLL FREE: 1-800-CAREER-1
FAX: 201-427-2037

Copyright © 1990 by Paul Kaponya

How To Survive Your First 90 Days At A New Company, By Paul Kaponya. ISBN 0-934829-56-X, $12.95

Copies of this volume may be ordered by mail or phone directly from the publisher. To order by mail, please in-clude price as noted above, $2.50 handling per order, plus $1.00 for each book ordered. Send to: The Career Press Inc., 62 Beverly Rd., PO Box 34, Hawthorne, NJ 07507

Or call Toll-Free 1-800-CAREER-1 to order using your VISA or Mastercard or for further information on all books published or distributed by The Career Press.

# Acknowledgements

## MY SPECIAL
## THANKS TO:

Although much of this book presents my personal observations and experiences, it would not have been complete without the contributions so graciously shared by my fellow Human Resources professionals, especially those members of the Personnel and IUNdustrial Relations Association Inc. (PIRA) of Southern California, many of whom are quoted throughout.

Special thanks to Ron Fry, president of The Career Press, for recognizing the potential value of the book for the men and women in our corporate halls who strive for lives of achievement and satisfaction. And for his ongoing help and encouragement.

Finally, my thanks to Larry Wood and Anthony Rutigliano, both at Career Press. Larry's incisiveness helped make the manuscript more cogent and meaningful. Tony's detailed editing was a masterful job, ensuring that the key points and advice I wanted so much to give were clearly and concisely elucidated.

# Dedication

## TO PAUL, JEFF, SHARI AND DARCI

Your mother, Joanie, your grandmother Arlynn, and I are so very proud.

We celebrate our kinship.

# Table Of Contents

# HOW TO SURVIVE
# YOUR FIRST 90 DAYS
# AT A NEW COMPANY

# Introduction

# WILL *YOU* SURVIVE YOUR FIRST 90 DAYS?

Whether you're entering the hallowed halls of the work-a-day world for the first time or are a longstanding veteran of the corporate highways and byways, your first days at a *brand-new* job will be some of the longest of your life.

You've suddenly entered an alien environment, a wholly-new landscape peopled with creatures you've never seen before—your new bosses, colleagues and, if you're lucky, underlings. No matter how many years you've spent striding confidently to and through boardrooms, you're suddenly forced to humbly ask the most basic questions—What time is lunch? Where's the bathroom?? How does this darn phone system work???

Congratulations! You're a freshman all over again, even if college is a long-dim memory.

Of course, you're anxious to get going. The way the job was described to you, the dynamics of what you see around you, the "welcome aboard" you've gotten—everything tells you that your anticipation is well-founded and your move well-advised.

But beneath that confident veneer, you can't help wonder if you're going to survive at all. You feel ignorant and are sure that everyone around you thinks you are!

Even after you get to know the ropes a bit, the pressure can be enormous. You are being initiated into a new culture. Whether and how you will "fit" into it won't become clear for about the first *90 Days* on the job.

Why *90 Days?*

The end of your third month at your new organization is a loaded date:

- *90 Days* is when most organizations review your performance.
- *90 Days* marks the end of probation at many companies, a time when they feel free to cut you loose if you aren't working out, even if they're basing that judgment on a hunch. (After such a probationary period, most organizations will not terminate anyone without cause.)
- *90 Days* is usually when the company must pay the recruiter who placed you at the firm. With search firms charging 20 to 30 percent of your first year's salary, you can bet the company will not pay such a hefty fee unless they're sure they want you around on Day *91*.

The central premise of this book is that the best way to survive the transition to a new job is to make sure the transition should be made at all. You can only figure this out if you know *who* you are and *what* your goals are. Therefore, the first two chapters help you build a Personal Inventory—a useful tool that will help you make the many important decisions about your working life you need to face.

Once you've decided it is indeed time to move on, the specific exercises in chapters 3-6 will help you choose the right *career,* the right *job* in that industry/career, the right *company* offering that job...and determine, before you waste time, whether the *boss* overseeing that promising job is someone you can get along with.

But, since getting there is only half the battle, the book certainly doesn't *stop* there. Chapters 7 & 8 discuss specific skills you will need to make the first 90 days—and beyond—happy and productive. And, in chapters 9 & 12, you will find advice on making great impressions on your boss and co-workers, managing time, and managing stress.

While this book is intended for anyone and everyone making the difficult transition to a new job, it addresses some specific concerns of graduating collegians—after all, many of you have never gone through anything like it before. So, for those of you really stepping out for the first time, chapters 10 & 11 will help cushion the "shock" of the transition from academia to "workademia."

This book is meant to give you a head start—to make you aware of actions that you can take before you cross the threshold of your new company to make your first 90 days on the job a springboard for success.

Use this book to put yourself in control of your career in the difficult years ahead. Those of you prepared for success won't have to keep looking back over your shoulder, wondering if your career is being sidetracked by others, by chance, or by the cosmic forces of change.

# 1

---

# DEVELOPING A PERSONAL INVENTORY: COMING TO TERMS WITH YOURSELF

---

We throw facts, ideas, theories at you. They have their place. But while you're trying to digest them, while you're busting your butts in courses the Outsiders don't give a damn about, you should be building a no-nonsense inventory of who you are, where you're going, and what you should be doing to get ready. We love you, but you're a bunch of Pavlovian Puppies. Why don't you insist college mix pure academics with what's of most import to *you* and what *you* want after graduation?

—Dr. Jim George, USC Dean, when asked to comment on the need for and value of a Personal Inventory.

**N**o doubt about it. This is one of the craziest times in your life. You're about to look for your first job or have decided it's time to try your luck at a new one. You're putting the finishing touches on your resume, scanning the classifieds, writing letters, calling everyone you know.

Then it's time to get ready for the interviews—with head hunters, personnel departments, prospective bosses. You prepare answers for all of the questions that are bound to come up.

Okay, so now you're ready to tell interviewers what they want to hear, present a package that you think they'll want to buy. You're all set, right?

Hold on a minute! Let's think about this.

When you're asked the most typical interview question in the world—"Where do you want to be five years from now?"—will *you* know the answer, really *know* it, not just be ready to trot out some pat response?

When an interviewer asks you for your strengths and weaknesses, will you be surprised and think to yourself, "Gee, what a good question!" Or will you be so sure of your response, so ready to knock 'em dead with a great answer, that the interviewer will be floored by your self confidence?

## Who Are You?

Granted, this might not appear to be one of the best times for self reflection, but there actually is none better. You are preparing to make one of the most important decisions in your life. Whether this is your first job or one in a series, make up your mind that it will be the *best* job you can get, the one that's *most* suited to your personality, the one that can help deliver what *you* want out of life.

The first step to accomplishing these seemingly lofty goals is to get to know yourself a little better. While this is absolutely essential preparation if you are steeling yourself to take that first shaky step away from school, it's never too late to learn about yourself. The following exercises are pertinent to everyone.

## Do You Know Yourself?

The following questions will help you to put YOU in perspective.

*Does the way you play a game, any game—sports, cards, Monopoly, etc.—say anything about the kind of person you are?*

Studies indicate that personality traits that show up in games correlate significantly with behavior in other non-game circumstances and to results from formal personality tests. Are you competitive in games? Or do you just tolerate them? What kind of loser are you? Whether its a physical or social game, do you hang in there to the bitter end? Or do you find yourself quitting, saying, "To hell with it" when things don't go well? The answers can be valuable as you plan your career path.

*Are you a stranger to yourself?*

A lack of self-awareness can cause insecurity, some confusion, and personality conflict. It's not too late, even if the stresses and pressures of academia have not allowed time for your assessment before graduation.

A disturbing question: *Have you found it harder to get acquainted with yourself than with co-workers, classmates, professors and others?*

"Yes," was probably your answer if you're like most of us...and honest. You should take a simple step to get to know yourself again: record your voice. Better yet, if it doesn't scare you, have a friend shoot a videotape of you being interviewed so that you can see yourself as others do.

Studies by the National Institutes of Mental Health show that your voice reveals a great deal about your personality and character. People are often surprised, even shocked or dismayed, when they first hear their own voices. Yet doing so can give you invaluable insights into what impact you probably have on those who can and will affect your career, your self-confidence or lack of it, your warmth or indifference, your empathy or unresponsiveness.

Okay, you've written down the answers to those tough questions. As your reward, you get to answer some more.

## Write It *All* Down

Here are some key questions to ask yourself. Write down your answers to help you formulate your "autobiography," an important part of your Personal Inventory:

- What successes did you have in school or on previous jobs? Which made you the proudest? How and why did you achieve these successes? In what ways do you think they may have a bearing on eventual career success?

- What kind of friends did you have early in life? Why did you select them as your friends? What kind of friends do you have today? Why did you select them as your friends? Which profs or bosses do (did) you like? Dislike? Why? In what ways do you think your selections and opinions have a bearing on the critical choices you will face regarding organization, job, boss?

- What failures do you recall most vividly? Why did they occur? What can you do to prevent them happening again? Looking back, were these mistakes helpful in avoiding similar setbacks in your career?

- What have been the disappointments in your life? Why? Goals are necessary, but were they attainable? Were your expectations—your own, others' —realistic?

- How do you react to people in authority—your parents, teachers, bosses? Do you think these reactions predict success/problems ahead? How?

- Were there any extracurricular college activities in which you were involved (the performing arts, debate society, politics, athletics, publications, clubs, fraternities) that offered clues as to what your best career choice might be? Have you, as humorist Art Buchwald did at USC, become involved in an activity that could portend high achievement in the "Real World?"

• Each of us has traits that could hold us back. Do you know what yours are? How can you modify them so they won't weaken your climb?

These questions will help you determine who you are and what you *really* want.

Remember. To get the most out of this exercise, write down your answers. Don't be concerned about language and writing skill. Answers can be a word or two, a few phrases, or complete sentences. At times you may end up with a page or two. The length of your answers is not important. But it *is* important that you be brutally frank and honest.

And as you focus on the past, don't look only for easily recalled, dramatic experiences and memories. Try to get a near-total picture. Look at the small details that stayed with you; if they recur when you think about the past, they are significant. Put them down, for they undoubtedly played a part in making you who and what you are today.

You will be surprised at the helpful results of this exercise.

## Don't Stop Writing Yet!

Having answered these questions, try this experiment during your first 90 days on the job: Begin a diary of significant events and your reaction to them. Don't ignore the off-beat, unusual events because you don't think they're "typical." "Oh," you may loudly proclaim, "That was unusual; that wasn't me at all; I'm really not like that." But analysis of what causes greater anger than we would admit to, or exhilaration beyond our fondest hopes, or depression beyond despair, may reveal much more clearly what and who we really are than any so-called "typical" experiences.

No matter how long these feelings last—a moment, an hour, a day—record them. What counts is that you *did* experience them, that they *did* have impact.

These questions will help you analyze your feelings. Think back: Do the experiences have a pattern? Are there certain individuals or types with whom you've consistently had problems? Why? Is it personality? "Chemistry?" A "Generation Gap" problem?

Are you experiencing resistance to authority? If so, why? Is the resistance justified because your superior's leadership style is not to your liking?

Is there a special kind of problem that recurs? Are there certain individuals or types with whom you like to work better? Why?

What is/was your role in each significant situation? Do certain actions on your part tend to promote your acceptance and favorable reaction? Are there any actions on your part that tend to create less than favorable reactions?

# If You've Still Got A Pad Of Paper

Here is another technique for getting to know yourself a little better. Write the following seven headings (one each) on seven sheets of paper—"My Needs," "My Ambitions," "My Interests," "My Personal Traits," "My Personal Activities," "My Experience," "My Training." The following questions will help you fill in these seven pages:

## Your Needs

Are status and prestige important to you? Do they overshadow desire for material wealth? Or are they neck and neck on your priority list? Do you agree with status-conscious types who claim, "You are what you drive?" and "Clothes make the person?"

Are authority and power important to you? Where on the list does "sense of accomplishment" belong? How about "psychic security"—love, affection, a feeling of being accepted? Is being part of an organization, a team you like and respect, paramount in your career plans? Or does going it alone appeal to you most?

## Your Ambitions

Do you really know where you want to go, and will you know when you get there? If you don't know where you're going, according to the old saw, any road will take you there.

List as many goals as you can—monetary, career, psychic. Detail the plans you have to achieve these. What is success—for you? Write down *your* definition. Then finish by completing the following sentences:

One year from now my plan says I would like to be _____
_____.

Three years from now my plan says I would like to be _____
_____.

Ten years from now my plan says I would like to be _____
_____.

Complete these sentences, ponder them, revise them. Then read the next chapter. It will give you ideas for a Master Plan that can make *you* the Master of your destiny. Finally, put the list of commitments into a Personal Inventory file—and keep a boiled down copy in your wallet as a prickly reminder.

## Your Interests

Write down those things that you really enjoy or think you'll enjoy about your career. Do you like to run your own show, or do you enjoy working within the confines of an organization?

Compare this list with your notes under "Needs." If you are organizationally inclined, what suits you most—working alone or in concert with others? Do you like a hustle-bustle, maybe even frenetic atmosphere? Or do you prefer a quiet, monastic corner where you can concentrate and cogitate uninterruptedly? Are you thing-oriented or people-oriented?

Interests are an important part of the foundation on which you build life goals. Don't underestimate their place in your choice of career, job, company and boss.

## Your Traits

Do you see yourself as a leader? How can you tell? List ten reasons you think you are, or can be, a leader.

Do you know what a leader needs to know and how to improve your leadership skills? In a later chapter, we will look at a controversial question: Are leaders born, or can they really be "made?" The answers will help you to decide your leadership potential.

An important trait you should identify is your sensitivity to people and *their* needs. Do you know how to act as a leader so people will give a damn and bust their butts for you? How about new ideas? What about flexibility, the ability to roll with changes? Does your self-image resemble what others see? What about your self-confidence level, especially after you have filled a page or two with answers?

Attach another sheet of paper to the "Traits" page and list 10 or 20 of your personality characteristics that you think may affect your prospects for success. Then, strictly from your own point of view, judge them as "No Problem" or "Problem".

The sheet will look something like this:

| TRAIT | NO PROBLEM | PROBLEM |
|---|---|---|
| Adaptability | X | |
| Enthusiasm | X | |
| Creativity | | X |

When you begin your job search, interviewers will quiz you about leadership—some of them mercilessly—since most organizations not only are intent on assessing your credentials for an immediate job opening, but also your potential for future jobs.

If they do not try to appraise your leadership potential during the job interview, you can bet that sooner or later you will face such interrogation. Give this section, and our later look at the leadership question, special attention.

Remember, too, that some people have failed as employees only to find magical doors opening to a richer life as entrepreneurs or small business owners. Corporate life isn't everyone's cup of tea.

## Your Preparation

Every form of training exposure you have had, formal or informal, should be listed. Don't overlook a single exposure: The one you skip may be the one you need the most.

Among my highly successful friends are many who benefited because they inventoried their training experiences and capitalized on them.

One friend is the chief operating officer and owner of a multi-million dollar electronics firm in the Midwest because his training in World War II gave him the confidence to launch a new career after floundering as an employee with employer after employer.

Another is a wealthy realtor in Southern California because he finally chucked his not-too-promising career as a purchasing agent and used the training as a real estate salesman gained during college vacations.

Still another is now owner of a highly successful accounting firm because he reviewed his training experiences. He realized that his college training, his part-time work as a bookkeeper while in school, his two years of accounting work after graduation, when added to his ability to get things done through people as a personnel administrator, would fill a greater need for others.

Once completed and analyzed, your list of exposures can: (a) move you on to new horizons or (b) goad you toward bettering your present position and (c) challenge you to determine what training you must consider today.

---

# Self-Knowledge
# Equals
# Self-Confidence

---

The more you know yourself, the more confident you will be that the choices you are making are the correct ones. By following the autobiographical suggestions in this chapter, you will be in the best position to influence, even control, your own future.

Evaluating yourself, however, is just the first step in this Personal Inventory process. It's also vital to get valuable feedback from others, an exercise that certainly will test your courage!

# 2

## How Others See You: Feedback For Your Personal Inventory

**W**ithout feedback, we couldn't develop. The criticism and praise we receive from parents and other authority figures shape our conscience and behavior. The desire we have for others to like us often determines our actions.

The feedback you've received your entire life has helped to create the YOU you've just tried to get to know a little better.

The goal of the last chapter was to get you to be introspective, to create a self-portrait. The goal of *this* chapter is to get you to find out how *others* really see you.

Combine this information with your self-portrait, and you will have a three-dimensional look at yourself, the best way to get to know your best and worst sides.

There are many reasons to do this, the most important of which is to minimize the effects of the almost inevitable disparities between "how I see myself" and "how others see me." Unrealistic personal inventories have time and again impeded or wrecked careers. I have seen countless people fired or demoted because their own inventory of personality and capabilities did not jibe with how others saw them.

You can get this feedback from many sources: professionals trained in psychology, career specialists, and, of course, trusted friends and family members.

And there is the source to which I will devote most of the chapter—the invaluable T-group experience.

# Sensitivity Training

Potentially the best opportunity available for developing self awareness, but especially for finding out how you relate with others, is sensitivity training.

No other feedback will help you evaluate your listening skills, the most important of your communication capabilities.

No other feedback can provide more meaningful insights for strengthening the single most important success element of your career—the ability to win friends and gain their support.

No other feedback can give you better indicators about your leadership ability, help you learn why people resist your leadership, how to overcome it, get them to bust their butts for you.

And no other feedback can give you better indications of the strengths and weaknesses in your temperament you should know about as you face the complicated maze of interpersonal relationships you will find in the career world.

Examine this feedback mechanism, evaluate it, check it out with those who have had the good fortune of experiencing it. Then schedule your participation at the earliest possible point in your career path.

## The Sensitivity Exposure

It goes by many names and there are many versions: T-Groups ("T" for "Training"), National Training Laboratory in Human Relations, Sensitivity Training, and so on. On a national scale, you may have heard of it as the Human Potential Movement. To avoid confusion, and because I think that it best describes the activity, I shall call it Sensitivity Exposure. If you are genuinely interested in developing a more complete personal inventory, you'll want to consider seriously this exciting, potentially valuable experience.

Methods vary. The method I can recommend had its basic origin at the National Training Laboratories in Washington, D.C., which for some time has arranged sessions each summer at Bethel, Maine.

NTL-type group experiences are available in most sections of the country, often sponsored by a university, but rarely, if ever, as part of the curriculum. Many corporations and other organizations, recognizing their potential value, now send hundreds of their executives and middle managers to T-groups each year.

## How T-Groups Function

A T-group is nothing like you've experienced before. You are thrown together with a heterogeneous group of people (usually about 25), a group that's as diverse as the raconteurs of *The Canterbury Tales*. That's it. No leaders, *per se*. No curriculum. No agenda. No goals.

I attended one at Santa Barbara a few years ago, arranged by UCLA. My particular T-group had a number of executives, educators, a housewife who insisted on being identified as a homemaker, a speech therapist, a psychologist, an editor, a Naval officer (who concealed his career ties from everyone but me), a just-graduated student, a head nurse, and a teacher.

Our group was plunged into a near-complete "unstructured" situation. There was no agenda and no leader. The only "structuring" was a number designated for the group, where we were to meet, the hours for sessions, theory sessions (lectures on human behavior, group dynamics, etc.), and cafeteria hours.

And, yes, there were two strange "participants" in the group to add a semblance of structure. Others vaguely referred to them as "staff" members. At one point, because some of our group felt threatened by them (among other reasons), we unceremoniously "rejected" them and asked them to leave us for a half day or so.

When a group sits down with neither agenda nor leader, strange things happen, whole new experiences develop, some of them rather shocking. A good part of that result is because the structure, or rather, the *lack* of structure, is so new to us. How often have *you* sat down at a conference table facing an utterly silent group of strangers, just staring at one another, uncomfortable, uncertain, perplexed?

It doesn't last forever. Sooner or later, someone in the group can't stand the pressure of silence. In our group, it was a fragile lady who, with an uncertain smile, shyly gurgled the first words: "Let's introduce ourselves." She was promptly clobbered because, in someone's opinion, "introductions would be incongruous." Others asserted, "We are in this new situation for interacting with one another, for relating and for venting our feelings, not for learning names!" Hostility had surfaced, and we were off.

## What You'll Learn

In the discussions, encounters, and confrontational experiences the T-group provides, you can discover why some people seem to like you, why others feel hostility, why some will listen, why others won't.

The experience may lessen the shock you will experience —sooner or later—out here in the Real World.

If you dare get involved, you can test your powers of persuasion, of leadership, of acceptance (or not) as a group member. You will find that one of your toughest challenges is to sell yourself and your ideas.

You may learn patience with groups, observing how people in unstructured situations experience a lot of pain and need time to develop a group feeling, a willingness to establish goals as a group and to act as a group.

You can learn much about your own toleration for frustration, especially if you are a go-go, task-oriented person who thrives on action and results. You will realize all too soon how individuals and groups take their time about decisions. You can, if your antennae are up, learn invaluable lessons about what makes a group tick.

If you observe behaviors and listen for meanings, not just words, you can experience one of the most important human relations experiences of your life. You will become more keenly aware of temperamental patterns, of reasons that people resist authority, change, conformity.

Perhaps never again in your life will you have a better chance to develop one of the toughest of all human relations skills—the art of listening. You learn after the first day to listen as you never have before, if for no other reason than "to survive." Not hearing it "like it is" can result in the group mercilessly attacking you. All of us must improve our listening skills. Like the alcoholic who begins his successful conquest of his disease only after he declares, "I am an alcoholic," you, too, will become a skilled listener only after you declare, "I am a poor listener."

# A Spreading Notion

Today a growing number of moves are afoot to explore the advisability of providing sensitivity exposures in school. Some colleges already provide a "partial" opportunity—UCLA, Stanford, University of Utah, and USC, among others. At USC, for example, Dr. Bob O'Donnell, while not following the T-group pattern, offers students sensitivity exposures in a class on Organization Behavior.

The value of these experiences is given credence by the story related by a recent graduate who was having trouble getting promoted at his job:

> The T-group experience helped me to look at myself as I never had before. I don't think I really changed very much basically—I still demand, *not*

ask, a man to do his best, and I have no patience
when a mistake is made the second time. But I
think I got to know myself better and to accept myself more as a demanding individual. So I was
better able to accept others, to trust them more, to
understand them more, and to fight them less.

But, above all, I think I did generate a little more
compassion.

Can people's insights into themselves and others change
in two weeks as a result of the T-group experience? For some, no,
but for most others, definitely yes.

## Bouquets and Brickbats

A man I know in Southern California is today President
and CEO of his company, although at the time of his T-group
experience he had been told there was little chance of his moving
farther up the corporate ladder. At the time, his superiors wrote
in his yearly evaluation, "Although your exceptional technical
competence has meant rapid promotions to your present responsibility in middle management, your inability to work coopera-
tively with peer executives as well as your inability to solve
problems with some of your subordinates mean you won't be
promoted again at this organization."

Occasionally the sensitivity exposure can create trauma,
as it did for a young naval officer in our group. Coming from the
highly structured, regimented life of the U.S. Navy, where just
about every phase of your life is neatly laid out, he almost went to
pieces on the third day. He was frustrated that the "group" was so
painfully slow in *becoming* a group. It didn't seem to have the
slightest trace of cohesiveness—his demands for action, his
requests to be heard, his suggestions for organizing all fell on
deaf ears, he thought.

Finally, he attacked: "This is a horrendous waste of time.
This inaction is intolerable. We haven't made a single decision in

two days. What good is all this? Most of you are a bunch of neurotics, here for kicks or whatever. I'm getting out of here!"

He stormed out and returned to the structured environment in which he was more comfortable. That was more than a
decade ago. I wonder what he thinks about today's rapidly
changing, much less rigid, military structure?

Some people criticize the encounter technique because people can experience "shake-up shock," as the naval man did. Such
occurrences, however, are very rare. The rationalization is, and
I think it is a good one, that if you nearly crack up or *do* crack up
in a T-group, you very probably would have reacted just as badly
somewhere else some other time...a time probably more damaging to career plans.

I can't guarantee that the T-group will do anything for
you. Or that you will enjoy it. Or that you won't think it a waste of
time. I do know that many hard-headed business organizations
who carefully watch their budgets have found an opportunity to
provide meaningful exposures for executives interested in self-
growth...and willingly paid for them.

I can also guarantee that many successful people I know
have benefited measurably from T groups.

That if you ever do participate—with an open mind—the
experience can shake you up in a positive way and greatly
increase the value of your Personal Inventory.

And that the T-group can be a life adventure so meaningful it will remain with you for the rest of your days.

# 3

# CHOOSING THE RIGHT CAREER

I am one of the blessed people of the universe, because I get to do work I adore with people I adore.

—Daniel J. Travanti, accepting his second Emmy award

Peak performers like Travanti have achieved the ultimate satisfaction—loving their work and the people with whom they do it.

Unfortunately, many people find themselves at the other end of the spectrum—they describe their work with crass four letter words. For them, much of life—but especially their work—is the pits.

This chapter and the three that follow will help you choose the right career and the right job. Each of these choices deserves very special attention on its own. Each demands, as you shall see, somewhat similar, yet very separate considerations.

The *Career* is a lifework, a chosen course of one's life in a particular pursuit. In some respects, it's a calling. And it is usually long term, although people do change careers, sometimes quite often.

The *Job,* on the other hand, is a specific work activity that is part of a chosen career. For some, it can be long term, like the career. Most people, however, change jobs several times in their lifetime; some, even more often.

# The Relative Importance Of Your Career

Few life decisions you make will have a more direct bearing on your chances for a satisfying life than the choice of career. Nevertheless, many people make it rather casually. As James Coughlin, president of a San Francisco-based career counseling firm, noted, "Most of our lives are spent on our careers. Unfortunately, most people pay less attention to choosing their careers than they do to buying their cars."

Most people considering a career move or recently graduating college fall into one of three groups. Which of these best describes you?

1. You are firm in your career selection. You're convinced you've made the right choice and that there's nothing you'd rather do.

2. You are tentative about the career path you've selected. Perhaps you "gravitated" toward the "selected" career—following a hunch or a special interest or a family tradition (or prodding) or because your parents "channelled" you into it.

3. You have not as yet chosen any career path. Or, if you're still in college, perhaps you are torn between stepping into the career world and the less-threatening, more comfortable choice of continuing as a student?

## Defining Your Commitment

No matter which group you fall into, you must take the first step toward making sure the career you choose (or have chosen) is right for you. It might sound simple, but that first step is to answer this question: "Why should I work?"

Psychologist Henry Levinson of the Menninger Foundation noted that work is not merely a means of subsistence—it's also a psychological glue. It is a paradox, simultaneously both curse and blessing. Some make work out of play; some make play out of work.

Certainly work is fundamentally a means for survival, but work-for-money is not enough. Indeed, when work is seen as nothing *but* a means of securing money, life can become dismal. Two bumper stickers (an essential medium of expression in California) I noticed not long ago sum up this unhappy situation. One read, "I owe. I owe. So off to work I go". The other put the same thought a tad more crudely: "Work Sucks, But I Need The Bucks."

But work should make you a Contributor, not just a Taker. Work should make you feel that you count, that you matter. It is a major social device for identification as an adult—"So, what do you do?" is often the first thing you're asked when meeting anyone new.

Go back and review the notes you took about your personal inventory, then answer this question: Why do *you* want to work? For money? Security? Status? Power? For Fun? To be famous? For personal satisfaction?

The answer to this question is—quite literally—vital. Dr. John Rowe of Harvard University Medical School says being happy at work may be as important as "anything physical" that we do to improve health and to live longer.

Why? Defining your commitment will reduce the odds of career success becoming life misery. It's hardly unusual for a therapist to have a number of patients who made it in the business world and then suddenly discover, in their '40s or '50s, discover that career success just hasn't lived up to its glowing press notices...or their youthful expectations.

And it's less and less unusual for psychologists to have similar patients in their mid-'20s. Richard Berry, a psychologist at the University of California at Berkeley who wrote a report on the phenomenon, says, "It's something like an accelerated mid-life crisis."

Dr. Berry's view of the problem is shared by many in the behavioral sciences and those of us in the business world who deal regularly with career problems. It has emerged because many young aspirants make career choices based on demand in the marketplace, on security-related reasons, or on reasons or actions perpetrated by parents, without *also* considering their own interests, needs, and views about work.

Take the case of John Richmond (not his real name), an attorney with the Internal Revenue Service. He had a very comfortable income and a level of job security not enjoyed by many. His position gave him status among friends and neighbors. But a growing restlessness with the sameness of his responsibilities made him increasingly unhappy. Almost perceptibly, each day became more dull, more of a drag.

John, although eminently successful, was eminently miserable. Success had not delivered the satisfaction and happiness he perhaps naturally thought it would.

Reviewing his previous training helped turn his life around. Working at a boatyard during summer vacations and on some weekends while in college, John had quickly graduated from gofer to skilled work hound, helping to build and rebuild boats. He had enjoyed working with his hands, experiencing a sense of satisfaction with work that was so close to his love of boating. Once he compared his current life with that long-ago experience, he ditched it all to set up a small boat-building/repair operation in Costa Mesa.

"I suffered a big cut in income for some time, and a bigger one in prestige, I suppose. But I'm glad I made the sacrifice. I'm pleased with what I'm doing. I didn't like the conflict, the prosecutor's stance I had to take. I'm only sorry I didn't choose right when I was still in college."

# Making It And Hating It

In a recent poll of 1,750 attorneys younger than 35, about 40 percent said they were dissatisfied with their jobs. The dissatisfaction stemmed mostly from stress—being pressured by deadlines, competition, and family commitments.

According to Delaware Law School Assistant Dean Gary Munnke, who conducted the survey, "There is a gap between what they *think* the law will be and what it *is*.."

Apparently, John has a lot of company—young professionals, men and women, who say they've made it but hate it. Their career choices were made because of security, or money, or whatever, to the exclusion of other important considerations.

Some had actually chosen a career from one or another list of the "Ten Hot Jobs Of The Coming Decade." Most of their changes weren't as dramatic as John's. But the pattern is the same: They succeeded, but never obtained the satisfaction they thought accompanied success. In their search for self-fulfillment, they switch positions, companies, specialties, cities. All to no avail.

## Expanding Your Personal Inventory

But you don't have to join or remain in the ranks of the miserable.

People can delude themselves. A shy person might convince himself that he wants to go into sales because it pays so well. An uncreative person dreams of becoming a director of marketing.

This is not to say that people should never aspire to positions for which they are not perfectly suited. But before they do, they *should* study their personal profiles to see if they have the right tools. Those who don't should seek the training, read the books, or get the experience necessary to fulfill that career desire.

Here are some more questions to help you get on the right career track:

- What kind of career advancement potential do I have?

- Have any personality characteristics surfaced that would give me the ability to become a fast tracker in my chosen career? Or are there some characteristics that could hold me back?

- In choosing a career, should I stay with my college major? Why? Should I consider another path, totally unrelated to my major, that might provide greater satisfaction?

- If I have not firmed up a career choice, what careers are open to me with my formal education and degree?

- How do my strengths match up with the career I have in mind? Would my weaknesses preclude success in the career I have in mind?

## Creating And Keeping Your Options Open

To avoid becoming a victim of the "I-made-it-but-hate-it" syndrome, keep open your career options.

Even if you are very firm about your career choice, you should investigate and evaluate other career paths that may roughly, even peripherally, use the same talents as your current choice. As the following true-life examples show, it is good insurance to create and keep your options open.

When I first interviewed Michel Bergerac shortly after he had graduated from UCLA, he was resolute: his only interest and love was sales and marketing. He was almost totally resistant to any other career path. A year or two later, when he and I reviewed his future plans, he decided to create an option—moving eventually into general management.

We channeled him into ITT Cannon Electric's management trainee program, which included participation in UCLA's Executive Program. Mike's was a wise decision. Creating a new option and keeping it open, he eventually was promoted to Manager, International Sales; then President, ITT Europe; then, CEO of Revlon. One year after his association with that firm, he became the world's highest paid executive.

Gene Howald was working as a roofer during his senior year at Ohio State, not at all confident about selecting his "right" career. "But one day when my fingers were nearly frostbitten," he remembers, "I decided there must be a better way". So he went to the Columbus employment agency, where, acting in a manner "unlikely" for a college grad, he asked to be interviewed for McDonald's management trainee program.

Most people would ask, "Why would anyone with a degree want to choose the fast-food business as a career? The days are long, employees are transient and distrustful, and competition breeds like wildfire. And, after handling these problems, the fast food operator has to face the American public—critical, itinerant, demanding.

How about Gene? His view was a trifle different: "I got started in the most exciting career I could have hoped for." After a 5-year stint with McDonald's, Howald became president of Volunteer Quality Foods, which has the Southern California franchise for Wendy's. He is in love with his career, and he's independently wealthy to boot.

The key to his success? Gene says it's his ability to see exactly what he wants. "This provides me with the impetus for the discipline required to achieve my dreams. I have always known exactly what I wanted."

Consider these additional valuable guidelines from this high achiever:

- He has divided his goals into three categories: 1. financial; 2. personal; 3. lifestyle.

- He writes down his goals. "By doing so", he says, "they become more of a reality to your subconscious mind. And then you start thinking about how you are going to accomplish them. You have to give yourself enough reasons to want to achieve the goals. Reasons make the difference."

## Spinning *Your* Wheel Of Fortune

Keeping your career options open can be a challenge, as the following true story demonstrates.

Shortly after receiving his marketing degree, Chris joined an organization that provides personalized mail production services to advertising agencies, retail stores, financial institutions and fund raisers. In short order, he achieved the highest rate of new account sales, became involved with various projects, and, less than two years after earning his degree, was earning the princely sum of $60,000 a year.

Most graduates achieving that salary level after less than two years on the job would purr with satisfaction. But Chris at that point decided that, having saved enough to handle it, he would now move into his long-range career option. He applied for acceptance as an MBA candidate with the prestigious, but very rigorous Darden Graduate School of Business Administration at the University of Virginia.

When Chris had one semester under his belt, his former employer contacted him and offered him a key managerial spot in the San Francisco Bay area...with a $130,000 salary.

Again, for most graduates I have known, an offer like that would have set their eyes to dancing. Chris was, quite naturally, elated. The flattering proposition was tangible evidence of the employer's high regard for his performance and potential.

But—you guessed it. He decided to complete his MBA studies. And Shari, his bride of but one month, seconded his motion .

Obviously, Chris and his young wife strongly believed in the principle of creating and keeping your options open. They knew the satisfaction that comes with commitment and the resolve to avoid becoming an "I-made-it-but-hate-it" victim.

# Should You Be Out On Your Own?

Of course, another fundamental decision is whether to cast your lot with an organization at all. Perhaps you should start or buy your own business?

I urge you not to consider the entrepreneurial route unless you can meet the basic tests I will present later in this section. And, even though you think you meet those tests today, you'd be better off joining an organization already involved in the activity/service/product around which you plan to build your entrepreneurial career so that you can:

- Learn the ropes;
- Check out in real-world fashion whether or not you are making the right decision;
- Learn what it means to be an employee—how they view their jobs, their bosses, their organization; the frustrations they experience; the kinds of management action that motivates them to become enthused, results-centered, and profit-minded.

## The Entrepreneur's Test

Before deciding on the entrepreneurial route, make sure you have good answers to the majority (or more!) of these questions:

*Do you have a sufficient bankroll to launch your enterprise?*

It is assumed you have done your homework and know the amount you need to avoid the first of the two biggest causes of failure: undercapitalization.

### *Do you have the needed know-how/experience your new venture demands?*

Lacking this is the *second* biggest cause of failure.

### *Do you feel super-confident about yourself and your service/ product?*

Good. Because if you're not, lack of self-assurance and fear of your ability to get something started on your own will leave you open to scams, and there are many of them.

### *Do you have general management ability?*

This includes knowing about and understanding such spooky-sounding things as cash budgeting and cash flow; how to hire, train and motivate; how to collect overdue accounts; when to refuse credit; establishing objectives and plans to achieve them; and so on.

### *Do you have the energy and willingness to work harder and smarter than you ever have before?*

### *Do you have available right now, before you make the leap of faith, a hard-nosed checklist that aligns your ambitions with some semblance of reality?*

### *Are you healthy?*

The rigors of entrepreneurship demand more energy and more ungodly hours than any organizational career path.

### *Do you really know the risks, the sacrifices, the disadvantages of being an entrepreneur?*

Yes, positive reasons for selecting the "right" career path should dominate your decision. However, no decision will serve you well unless you also consider the negatives and pitfalls, so you can go into it with eyes wide open. Try to visualize the three very worst possible developments. Then—and only then—make your move.

*Do you enjoy working alone, making your own decisions, sinking or swimming with them?*

Initially at least, running your own show can be a very lonely proposition.

*Do you have the know-how to manage time, so it doesn't manage you?*

*Do you have the guts to conduct a no-nonsense review of your ongoing performance?*

In progressive organizations, a supervisor reviews how you're doing. Checking this against your own appraisal then gives you a pretty good idea of your strengths and areas that need improvement. And, if you're lucky, you'll get some helpful coaching.

Not so when you're on your own. Though you may check with others on questions from time to time, you are it—how tough and realistic your performance review of yourself is can easily mean the difference between success or failure.

*Do you have proof?*

I mean *genuine* proof that you are a self-starter who'll stop at nothing to be up and at 'em? In an organization, the would-be achiever has a combination of inner-induced and outer-induced propellants to prod him. When you're on your own, you must prod yourself. How well and how consistently you do that will determine whether you're a winner or loser.

*Do you relish taking risks?*

Do you know how far to go with risk taking?

*Is job security very important to you?*

Or could you adapt well to the insecurity of going on your own? Psychological experiments indicate that people who need job security have temperaments which they themselves describe as cooperative, determined, deliberate, efficient, stable.

On the other hand, people who are willing to take business chances in their stride and who do not value job security highly describe themselves as courageous, imaginative, important, clear-thinking, sharp-witted, ingenious and foresighted.

Give this temperament question some extra thought. Compare it to the personal inventory sheets you have developed, and you might do what Jeff Peters, a member of our family, did.

After his graduation from USC, Jeff joined a leading recycling firm. After surviving his first 90 days on the job, he moved rapidly up the pay scale. His performance earned him a promotion and a transfer to the East Coast.

A year later, however, he began to experience a growing restlessness. He reviewed his personal inventory and realized that the strong entrepreneurship interest he had developed in his undergraduate days (he had taken a two semester course in the go-it-alone activity) was beginning to bug him. He made some preliminary plans and contacts and, within weeks, resigned.

The company president, thinking that Jeff missed the West Coast, offered to effect a transfer and pay his moving costs. But Jeff was now firm in his commitment. He made the big change.

The enterprise with which he is involved is successful, but his response when I asked him about the venture was significant: "Instead of dragging myself out of bed each morning with a questionable level of enthusiasm, I now wake up at 4 or 5 in the morning, raring to go, take on all comers, work my butt off. It's a great feeling!".

## What You Can Look Forward To

The satisfactions, the money, the power, fame, or whatever you're looking for *is* there for the taking when you're an entrepreneur. Witness the results of a study of independent entrepreneurs:

- Asked how much money it would take to get them to accept a position as an executive or employee in someone else's organization, 58 percent answered that there was *no* amount of money that could induce them to make such a change. Another 28 percent imposed such wildly unrealistic conditions on such an offer as to effectively bar any chance of their being accepted.

- Asked what they would do if they lost their current enterprise, 72 percent replied that they would start another. (Many already had at least one failure.)

Testimony enough to pursue this career path if you feel *you* have the right stuff!

## A Place For Career Counseling

If you're still uncertain after going through some of these exercises that you're ready to choose a career, consider going for some career counseling. I am personally acquainted with three outstanding groups—at Marquette University, USC and UCLA.

Career counseling can be particularly valuable if you are:

- Undecided about your life's work;
- Not altogether certain your choice of occupation is a wise one;
- Weighing the option of further education or training;
- Dissatisfied with progress in your first job;
- Are encountering difficulties in the critical first 90 days on the job;
- Concerned about what to do for personal growth within your chosen career.

The process goes something like this:

Preliminary interviews with your counselor cover your specific questions and background information related to your career.

Tests are administered that will help you and your counselor study your preferences, needs, strengths and weaknesses.

This is a golden opportunity to check out your own personal inventory.

Analysis and discussion of your background data and test results help you understand yourself and your potential for growth—personal and career. This includes a discussion of your chosen career or other career options appropriate for your special circumstances.

About 20 to 25 hours are involved, spread over a period of time convenient to you, but usually not exceeding three months.

If you want to be a peak performer and avoid the "I-made-it-but-hate-it" syndrome, you must give career plans hours of thought. Do so before you make your first or next career move. And be committed to keeping your options open.

You'll be glad you did.

# 4

# CHOOSING THE
# RIGHT ORGANIZATION

I felt great from the very first day I was on the job.
Everyone seemed to welcome me, and they seemed
to really care about getting me off to a good start.
I'm glad I passed my probationary period. This is
where I want my career to be.

There's no way I'm going to stay with that creepy
company. I'm getting the hell out of there. What a
basket of snakes. Instead of working together,
everybody looks for ways to knife each other. And I
don't know what's expected of me. So where does
that leave me?

The first quote is from a college graduate I recommended
for hire by a Southern California aerospace firm following a
campus recruitment trip.

The second is from an interview with a college graduate referred to me for career discussions by his father, a fellow executive. The father feared that his son's attitude, and *not* the organization he had joined, was at the root of the problem. In fact, it *was* the organization that was at fault.

These quotes demonstrate that how well you fare when you step over the threshold to your new job depends largely on the kind of organization you've chosen.

# Where Lilacs Bloom...
# And Where They Die

In Wisconsin the lilac bush is everybody's favorite plant. Nature blessed it with delicate, lustrous colors and a very special fragrance. The lilac's brief but brilliant presence on Spring's splashy stage is always a welcome event.

But plant the same bush in Southern California and the lilac's springtime entrance becomes a non-event. Bearing only a slight resemblance to the Wisconsin variety, the lilac in California's Southland is just another bush. It doesn't grow to its proper height. Its blossoms are a pale version of the northern variety. And the heady aroma is missing.

There is an important corollary here: As with the lilac, your career will grow, flourish, and become a successful presence in some environments; in others, it can become a non-event.

Choosing the right organization will increase your chances for staying in control of your career track and not allowing accident, circumstances, and fate to exercise undue, unwelcome influence.

You must investigate various sources, both inside and outside prospective employers, to make sure that you are choosing the right place to begin your career.

# Outside Sources Of
# Company Information

The local *Chamber of commerce* can be a helpful source if your target company is out of town. It will give you whatever information it has about the organization you have in mind.

Does the Chamber know the organization's reputation in employee relations? If there is a union? Has the company been struck often? Hardly? Is the company a member? If the Chamber issues lists giving the rank of companies by dollar volume, what position does your outfit occupy? Is it increasing or decreasing?

*Business/industry associations:* The same and other questions can be posed to these sources. Your target(s) should belong, if they amount to something in their industry. Most cities also have general associations, such as the Merchants & Manufacturers Association in L.A. and the California Manufacturers Association.

Then there are technical and professional groups in most major industries that also can become an excellent resource.

*Your personal contacts:* For openers, get in touch with a friend who was formerly employed by the organization or a friend of a friend who may have some information. This *is* a small world. Create a network of contacts and make the most of them.

*Your predecessor:* The organization's interviewer may be shocked when you ask. But if you are genuinely convinced that the stakes are high, that it is important to cast your lot with the right organization, you will politely ask for the name of the individual who held the job for which you are interviewing and how you can contact him. If the individual was transferred or promoted, so much the better. Ask if it's okay to chat with him.

If the answer is no, you will have learned a lot, right? If yes, you'll be able to weigh responses to your questions about the organization from an ex-employee against you impressions. Getting to know what exhilarated, bugged, disappointed or enraged him may fill in some key parts of your jigsaw puzzle.

*Some executive, professional and technical placement agencies:* These may have limited but helpful information about the organization's climate, preferences for leadership style, etc. Some have very intimate knowledge about these things.

*School alumni:* Your placement office, fraternity/sorority, or alumni association may give you the lead you need to identify someone inside the organization or a former employee. Also, if the organization is located in the school's general area, you may find what you need from a faculty member in the Business Administration School.

*Business editor:* Few people in a community, large or small, are more knowledgeable about organizations than the town's newspaper business reporter or editor. Although they're busy, if you approach them properly, they are generally an understanding lot.

I know of several situations in which graduates were so impressed with the objective, hard-nosed views expressed by the editor that the information obtained played a key role in their decision-making process.

In fact, I recall three cases in which the graduates were so impressed with views expressed by the press that they flatly turned down what outwardly appeared to be desirable, high paying jobs. One of these involved a graduate who had been heavily recruited on campus, wined and dined and made to feel wanted with an annual salary level $5,000 above the nearest offer.

*Publications/directories*, such as:

— *Dun & Bradstreet's Million Dollar Directory*

— *Dun & Bradstreet's Middle Market Directory*

— *Dun & Bradstreet's Reference Book of Corporate Managements*

— *Encyclopedia of Associations, Volume 1: National Organizations (Gale Research Co.).*This lists organizations that are in the business of giving information—very helpful if you want to check out a choice potential employer in another state.

— *F & S Index of Corporations and Industries*. This lists published articles by industry and company name. Updated weekly, this not only can help you check out an organization, but also become better prepared for your final job interview—and impress them with your knowledge of the organization. More often than not, companies that have articles published are movers, leaders or potential leaders.

— *Fortune Magazine's 500* . If your target is on the list, it may have important information for your assessment. Reminder: Just because an organization is on the prestigious list is no guarantee it's the right company for you. Big certainly does not always mean better.

— *Standard & Poor's Register of Corporations, Directors and Executives*. Listed are key executives in 32,000 leading companies. If you are truly in earnest, you'll use such lists in the network you build to discover sources of information.

There are a number of other corporate directories available. Consult your local library and, especially, its reference and business sections.

# Getting Information From The Company Itself

*Annual reports:* Read the direct message and what's between the lines. The annual report does more than tell you about products or services, about the financial picture, the market position. Examine especially what the company's plans are, what accomplishments it's proudest of. Later you can use this information to compare answers to questions you ask during the job interview.

Note, too, what the annual report says about the "people" end of the business. It will give you clues about how *you* may be treated, whether you're going to be a number or a somebody. If the organization gives little or no space to the human resources aspect of the enterprise, chances are that's just the way it is, day-in, day-out—people get short shrift.

*Employee handbook:* You should ask for this potential gold mine of information. It does more than tell you about what the organization promises to do for you. If it was properly done, it will indicate what the organization expects from you.

*Sales/marketing brochure(s):* While this publication is not likely to offer answers to most questions you need for making the right choice, it can provide insights about the organization's professionalism and potential in the marketplace.

## What To Ask Your Potential Boss

The following questions should be posed with discretion, in a non-challenging manner. Preface them with a statement like this: "This is an important job opportunity for me. I would appreciate your patience and understanding about certain questions I have in mind. I want to get off to a good start."

That should give you a pretty good idea about laying the groundwork. Take it from there; do your own thing. Ask your potential supervisor:

*How would you describe the organization's financial condition today?*

The cash flow is? Accounts payable are? Have financial goals been on target? (Answers should give you at least good hints about the financial health of the organization.)

*Would you please describe the people in your organization?*

I'd like to know a little about the men and women with whom I would be working.

*How would you describe the organization's strengths? Weaknesses?*

Valuable information may emerge here for your assessment—information you may be able to check out with other sources.

*How would you compare this organization with others with which you have been associated or are familiar?*

What he stresses will give you additional hints. Watch especially for his enthusiasm level -- or the lack of it.

## What To Ask Campus Recruiters

Recruiters are highly skilled interviewers. They dig in depth quickly and efficiently to establish data for their decision making. If you ask the right questions, however, you are less likely to be mesmerized by an articulate, enthused recruiter.

The recruiter has a number of "knock-out questions" that, if not answered satisfactorily by you, can mean virtually immediate disqualification as a candidate. But *you* can arm yourself with your own "knock-out questions" that, if not answered to *your* satisfaction by employer representatives, can disqualify the organization for your further consideration. Here are some sample questions that can help you make the right choice:

*Who will make the final hiring decision?*

If the campus recruiter, a personnel department representative, or some person other than the individual to be your boss is given authority to say, "You're hired!" say, "Thanks, but no thanks."

An organization that doesn't insist that a boss must personally hire all his subordinates is just not with it. Or, if your would-be-boss is "too busy" or doesn't think it's necessary to fulfill this vital managerial responsibility himself, he has problems, problems that can detrimentally affect your career once you're hired. Further, there's always the chance he may second guess the person who selected you; you may then be licked before you start.

*How have graduates from other years fared?*

Ask your interviewer(s) to tell you about former students from your school who cast their lot with the outfit. How did they fare with promotions and otherwise? Ask for their names, year of graduation, and where they can be reached.

The organization will be investigating you, so why not investigate them, too? With such information in hand, aren't you in a better position to approve the organization?

Another salutary effect of such information, of course, is that interviewers will be less inclined to distort and oversell.

### Is the company willing to put in writing all details of the employment offer if one is made?

If they are in any way fuzzy or vague about pay, progression opportunities, position, title, job content, moving and travel expenses, and other considerations, you can be sure they'll be even more fuzzy and vague after you begin employment.

It's simply good business to put in writing all conditions that relate to your hire and your future.

### Is the organization willing to outline your job responsibilities?

And does it guarantee challenges you can really sink you teeth into?

A position description—*at least* a job summary—should be available. Only with that as a reference can you dig enough to determine the challenge content of your work in the organization.

Due to talent shortages, many companies develop and maintain a "skills bank," hoarding talent until needed. In some situations, this may be to your benefit, but remember that a year or two of marking time can hasten your technical and managerial obsolescence in this day of rapid change.

### Which promotion ladder of the organization did key executives climb?

Did the top people move up from Finance? From Production? From Marketing? Elsewhere?

If your ambitions include reaching a rung at or near the top, you can pretty well validate your chances. You already know your own field of activity. If it calibrates with the promotion history of the firm, you have a chance.

### What is the organization's policy on transfers?

Tens of thousands of executives move each year. Mobility in many corporate quarters has become a must for career success. You must consider how many, if any, moves *you* are willing to make in the next ten years.

Then ask the organization how hard-nosed *they* are about moves? Is there a minimum or maximum number of moves for each individual? Does the first refusal immediately knock you out of future promotional consideration? The second? Suppose after making five moves you refuse the sixth? What happens to your career?

Some graduates I know have moved three times in a four-year span.

***What does the organization mean when it calls itself "progressive"?***

"Progressive" can be a meaningless abstraction, useful as a propaganda tool by interviewers to snare your interest.

It's also important to determine what *you* mean by a "progressive" organization, then dig to determine whether the prospective employer's version of "progressive" is compatible with yours.

## Is The Company People-Oriented?

All organizations *say* they are, but the sad fact is that most *aren't*. To ascertain your prospective employer's commitment to its people, you must plan your questions carefully.

Many organizations and their officials know how to articulate the principles of sound personnel management. Often, however, practice does not measure up to what is preached.

To get a good picture of a company's People Quotient, some of the following questions may help:

***What is the turnover rate in the group to which I would belong?***

And what is the rate among executives?

Often these figures serve as a good barometer for determining employee satisfaction or lack of it. Turnover figures vary somewhat by industry. One guide, however, is to proceed with caution if the annual turnover percentage is more than three percent. If it is more than five percent, proceed with extreme caution. If near or over ten, don't proceed at all. Chances are good you will become merely one more part of the revolving door group.

***Does the organization have policies for handling employee problems?***

How have these been communicated?

The effort to implement such policies, and practices related to them, will tip you off as to the company's attention to its people. As a result, you may perhaps be able to classify the company's " People Quotient" as: (a) "High and genuine;" (b) "measurably evident and reasonably sincere;" (c) "negligible and rather superficial;" or (d) "couldn't care less."

***Does the organization conduct management appraisals?***

If the company has a formal program to evaluate promotability among employees, you can be reasonably sure it encourages personal growth, that you won't be lost in the shuffle, and that politics will have a minimal effect on promotional opportunities.

## Check With the Placement People

If your alma mater's placement people take their work seriously, they should have helpful information available which would tend to verify or discount what you've been told by company recruiters, and to help you evaluate your personal impression of the firm.

In addition to general information about its "corporate climate," your school's placement people should know how company representatives have conducted themselves during campus recruitment campaigns. Do they keep promises? Were they gentlemanly in the fierce battle for recruits? Or do they take the end-justifies-the-means approach?

# Want The Answers?
# Ask the Right Questions!

Scientists have proven that finding a solution to a problem consists primarily in asking the right question in the right way—and, often, at the right time. On the other hand, they will also tell you that if you persist in asking the wrong question, or don't ask any, you cannot hope to move ahead.

Apply this valuable lesson to the problem of trying to select the organization that is best for you. Listen, and listen with a selective, critical ear when companies interview you, but also conduct your own examination—by asking pointed questions in interviews and using all available outside sources before making the crucial decision.

## Look For Telltale Clues

You should also be careful not to overlook other signs that will indicate whether or not an organization is right for you..

Take the case of Bob Cannon. He could look another in the face, anytime, anywhere, because he always put the saddle on the right horse. People trusted him.

However, as president of Cannon Electric Company after his founder father died, he realized that it was not enough. He learned fast that an effective leader must sound the clarion call that tells his followers the route he'd like to see them take. So, after many discussions with me (he liked to remind me once in a while: "Paul, since you're Vice President of Personnel I want you to be the conscience of this organization" ) and other key executives, Bob developed a set of principles for his organization, which I've reproduced on the next page.

They are not mere words, but a public commitment, a way of life that made work a satisfying experience. Those principles served as a polestar, creating for Cannon's people an enviable corporate climate, one that did indeed encourage growth.

TO DEVELOP an organization of exceptional people possessed of respect for the dignity of the individual and imbued with the spirit of the team.

TO PROVIDE a facility with which we can produce to our utmost in an efficient and pleasant environment.

TO DEVELOP and produce products of such quality, and render such service, that we may always be proud of our efforts.

TO MARKET the product of our endeavor at a reasonable profit for continuing growth, reward for effort and a return on investment.

TO ACCEPT our responsibility to our community, our country, and our fellow man.

These are our principles

— Cannon Electric Company, Since 1915

Cannon's principles are the kind of telltale clues you want to look for. Ask your prospective employer about any statements of intent or policy that exist.

Discovering telltale clues is not enough, however. You must check them out. Listen to all the glowing descriptions and promises recruiters offer but *check them out with hard questioning, sort out the positives and negatives.* Float in a sea of doubts today, so tomorrow your ship won't sink.

A plaque in the president's office carries a message he wants emphasized again and again. Invariably, the message also appears on the office walls of subordinate executives, in the employment office, strategically positioned so you have to catch a glimpse of it. Here is one plaque I saw on the wall of a CEO:

# What Is Hustle?

<u>Hustle</u> is doing something that everyone is absolutely certain can't be done.

<u>Hustle</u> is getting the order because you got there first, or stayed with it after everyone else gave up.

<u>Hustle</u> is shoe leather and elbow grease and sweat and missing lunch.

<u>Hustle</u> is getting prospects to say "yes" after they've said "no" twenty times.

<u>Hustle</u> is doing more for a customer than the other guy is doing for him.

<u>Hustle</u> is believing in yourself and the business you're in.

<u>Hustle</u> is the sheer joy of winning.

<u>Hustle</u> is being the sorest loser in town.

<u>Hustle</u> is hating to take a vacation because you might miss a piece of the action.

<u>Hustle</u> is heaven if you're a hustler.

<u>Hustle</u> is hell if you're not.

I found myself in agreement with most of "Hustle." But how about you? Suppose you observed this "Hustle" message on the wall during an interview. Would your reaction be: "Hey, this outfit has a bunch of doers, they'll go places."

Or would you think: "That view fits me to a T, but I don't know about that not taking a vacation or that 'hint' about no lunches."

Or maybe: "Hustle? Of course, but it's not hustle, but *how* you hustle that counts!"

Then too, maybe you should ask, "Is the author of 'Hustle' a workaholic? Does that mean I'll have to be one to succeed in this organization?"

## Ferreting Out Problems

Here are some other questions that will help spot potential trouble and identify special opportunities you might encounter at the prospective organization:

*How does this organization rank within its special activity/ industry?*

Pose this question to your interviewer(s) to check out information you gathered from other sources suggested previously in this chapter.

*Has the organization conducted an employee opinion poll?*

If so, how long ago? Ask if you could see some of the results..

*Are the company representatives you met outgoing?*

Did they make you feel genuinely welcome? Or did they seem cool, noncommittal? Are their faces smiling, happy, promising? Or strained, hinting the squeeze is always on, that the organization relies on pile-driver force to reach goals?

Don't underestimate the value of these impressions.

*What's attracting me to this company?*

This question actually involves interrogating yourself—taking a close look at You as well as the organization that sparks your interest. What has impressed you the most? Is it the organization's work? Its reputation? Your job there? The people, boss, peers? Professional climate? Promotional opportunities? Big dollars and other executive goodies in the offing?

If the latter looms as the biggest attraction, be careful!. Money is wonderful; it can make life exciting. But in the long run, most people find that to make it all worthwhile, they must like their work and the people with whom they must work, respect their organization, and enjoy a sense of achievement.

Look again at the organization that has especially impressed you with its lush economic package. Will it, in addition to giving you the wherewithal to purchase symbols of outer success, also help you to meet the real test of a meaningful life—using your talents to accomplish worthy goals?

### In what ways does the organization encourage personal growth and promote employees' educational training?

Does it have an educational refund plan? Would you be included?

### What is the quality level of the communication process?

How many channels have been developed? Used? Do people feel they are in the know? Are surprises kept to a minimum?

*No* organization can long endure as a healthy, viable entity without a sound information effort using effective communications tools. Without it, people are not happy, not dedicated, not satisfied...and your lot would be the same.

### Is the organization family owned?

What effect will this have on promotions? Are they likely to sell out? If they're swallowed by a larger organization, chances are good you'll be purged.

Is the company's financial structure sound? Some family-owned companies are loaded; others are thinly structured.

### What political situations exist?

Any takeover, merger or proxy fights in the offing? Change often threatens the health of your career, so if you can detect a major ownership/power change, be on guard.

### Is the company publicly owned?

If so, by all means check it out with an investment broker. You can, if you select the right one, learn more than just the price of the stock—the confidence, or lack of it, in future progress, managerial competency, etc.

## Real World Horror Stories You Want To Avoid

If you think you would enjoy the "comforts" of an outfit that lays down *all* the rules that will govern your life;

If you would welcome a thick manual that "guides" all your actions, including maybe how to flush the executive washroom toilet;

If you feel it's okay for an organization to request that you spend one-third of your time developing reports that shall include True Confessions detailing why some goals weren't met, some problems unsolved;

If you admire an organization that promotes political infighting to test the mettle of its career aspirants, that uses shredding machines to cover its tracks, that says the good of the organization is served best at times by muzzling its employees;

Then all you must do is adopt The Evel Knievel syndrome. Throw caution to the winds. Ignore the dangers. Put your career in the hands of fate. And if you find the organization I have described, well, you deserve each other. There are enough of these around.

However, if you want to avoid such an outfit like the plague, use the probing methods I have suggested. Get the lay of the land, pry, paw over the affairs of the organization the best you know how.

# 5

## CHOOSING THE RIGHT JOB

My God, Paul, there's got to be a better way to make a living!"

—Response to my "How are you?" from a brilliant executive in his early thirties. His salary is near the six figure mark and he is enjoying perquisites that are the envy of his friends in other corporations.

What do I like best about this company? My job. I knew long before I was graduated from college which career I wanted, but only after two big mistakes did I find the *job* I like—this one. I had almost the same activities in the other two jobs as on this one, but both of them were nightmares. In this job, I've got what I've always hoped for—like freedom to act, day-in, day-out, and written broad parameters. I like how the job here is regarded as important, and I know it can lead to bigger things. This job is great. The other two were for the birds.

—Response to a questionnaire from an employee opinion poll I conducted for a corporate client.

The second person quoted here is to be envied. What a wonderful situation—the right job in the right career! That's the ultimate in employment satisfaction and contentment!

However, if *you're* in a job that you don't like, or if you're about to graduate and feel enormous pressure to pick right the first time, keep the following facts in mind:

- According to a study by the National Bureau of Economic Research, most workers hold about ten jobs in their lifetimes.

- Most people, the study reveals, changed jobs four times before the age of 24.

- Between the ages of 25 and 39, the average person holds another four jobs. After 39, most people have fewer than three jobs.

- Highly-educated workers have a dropout rate that, in some respects, is worse than that of blue-collar workers. A random sample by Massachusetts Institute of Technology professor Dr. Edgar H. Schein showed that five years out of MIT, 73 percent of graduates had left their first jobs.

While these facts might have convinced you that you're probably not signing on to a job for life, you must be prepared to ask prospective employers some rather tough questions.

# What To Do Before
# The Job Interview

One of the most important steps to take before any job interview is to review your personal inventory. Undoubtedly it will suggest areas you will wish to probe during the job selection process.

For example, you might want to ascertain whether or not leadership skills will be required. Not everyone has the qualities successful leadership requires, nor does everyone aspire to leadership.

Career professionals will tell you it is a rare day when you can find a super salesman who also is a super leader. And the same goes for the bright, reliable engineer, the brilliant accountant.

Then be ready to ask the tough questions—I've given you sixteen in the next section. When posing these questions, do so in a matter-of-fact, non-aggressive manner. Most professional interviewers, I can attest, rarely are asked such pointed questions. Some may actually be shocked at your audacity. Yet you *must* pose these questions if you want to choose The right job.

If you perceive inordinate resentment and/or a reticence to provide the answers you need, you're probably better off crossing the potential job off your list (unless your evaluation of the organization and potential supervisor is otherwise favorable).

However, keep in mind that in most situations, if you handle your questioning discreetly, your investigative attitude will be a plus to your candidacy.

## 10 Key Questions To Ask Employers

*Is there an accurate written position description available that presents major activities involved and results expected?*

If one does not exist, write down what interviewers tell you about the job. Unclear, not fully understood responsibilities predict problems ahead—for you.

*To what other jobs at the company does this one lead?*

What have been the career paths of others who've started out at this position?

*Is the job in a class, department, or activity (sales/ marketing, management information services, finance, production, engineering, etc.) that has had a history of promotions up the corporate ladder?*

When asking this question, *do* avoid making a mistake common to many of today's graduates—communicating that you expect accelerated upward movement. Doing so can erode your chances.

### *Is income advancement based on merit?*

How often will my performance be reviewed? How often are performance reviews conducted? Remember, the most successful companies invariably have the best salary levels.

### *Will the job in its initial phases entail working alone, or will I be a member of a team?*

### *What are the people whom I will be working with like?*

The interviewer's level of enthusiasm when he answers this question might give you important clues.

### *Can you provide a complete list of perquisites?*

This will help you determine not only the total income package involved, but also the importance the organization puts on it. In almost all organizations, different job levels provide different benefits.

### *Does the job belong to a group that is included in a management appraisal/inventory program?*

Such programs identify those who are promotable, so the organization can have an inventory of its management talent. Such a formal program ensures you won't get lost in the shuffle, guarantees you a periodic appraisal of your potential, and, most likely, will involve follow-up efforts to improve your promotability.

### *Would you recommend this job to a member of your family you like, one who would qualify?*

If the interviewer answers affirmatively, ask: "Why?"

## 6 Key Questions To Ask Yourself

*If the job offer were withdrawn after I accepted it, would I really feel disappointed? Why?*

*If I were to accept the job, would I feel it is the best job offer I could have gotten?*

*Do I feel the job will use at least some of my talents?*

Remember that *most* entry-level jobs may at first appear too basic and simplistic. Often when a graduate begins in such a job, he may be initially assigned to a routine, non-challenging, non-rewarding set of "apprentice" duties.

If you have probed for details of the position and what is expected of you, are you fully convinced that temperamentally and motivationally you are suited to tolerate and cope with those entry-level duties for several months, maybe even a year or two?

Just as important—try to determine at what juncture you will have an opportunity to take on heavier assignments.)

*Am I absolutely sure this job will not require transfer to another geographic area not to my liking?*

*Does the job, though it's in my general career category, require any special skills in which I am weak or don't presently have?*

Will this lack detrimentally affect my chances for success right from the onset?

*Among the job openings for which I applied and am being considered, is the job I now feel inclined to accept the first, second or third choice on my list?*

After you have completed all the interviews for a particular job (you probably will have at least two for each), review the questions above. Then make yourself honestly rate that company's answers (questions 1—10) or your reactions to the company/job (questions 11—16). Give the company a grade for each question—"favorable" or "unfavorable."

Then total up all the "favorables" and give that company one point for each. If the company scores:

...14 to 16 Points: Congratulations. Although this score will not guarantee success, it indicates that you will choose wisely if you accept the job offer. Your chances are good for job satisfaction. The job, if you also select the "right" boss and "right" organization, will be an adventure.

...12 to 13 Points: A misadventure is possible. Be cautious. Be your best friend. Don't kid yourself. Reexamine each question and your responses. Consider all circumstances that surround the job. Weigh the pros and cons. .

...less Than 12 Points: Don't take the job if offered, unless hunger, a desperate financial condition, or very bleak job outlook leaves you no choice. If you do take it, do so with one thought in mind: "Unless very positive changes develop, this job is strictly an interim compromise until some day I find a 14 to 16 Point opportunity."

# Location, Location, Location

How important is location in your effort to land the right job? Very!

The experiences of too many disappointed ex-employees indicate the location question is far more important than most realize. It is especially crucial for graduates going out into the market for the first time.

While it is true that your opportunity to exercise selectivity is reduced in direct proportion to the extent that you limit your geographical availability, you must be concerned about location.

Have you really selected the right job if, after a time, the area in which you must live and work makes you miserable?

Hardly. The time to take a hard look at location is *before* you make a job choice, and this can mean looking at a dozen or two vital considerations that will fall into two general categories—personal and economic.

## Personal Factors That Make
## The "Where" Question Important

If you are a Type A personality (highly competitive; aggressive;achievement-oriented; a high-energy go-getter with a need to control), your best job locale—your personal Paradise—is the high-action, big city—New York, Los Angeles, Chicago, Houston, but in no event smaller than, say, Milwaukee or Indianapolis. You will simply not be happier in any "smaller" environment.

If you are a Type B personality (lacking a strong time urgency and hostility; possessing an ability to work and rest in a relaxed way; evincing a more "laid back" style in everything you do): Because your behavioral tendencies are less fixed and probably under better control, you can choose *any* size city.

In your situation, the biggest challenge is not so much where, though sooner or later you would probably dislike the pace of the big city. It is far more important that you exercise extreme care in selecting the "right" boss. As a Type B, you must avoid like the plague the frenetic organization and boss—places in which time is an endemic disease and people use pitchforks to motivate.

My experience over the years tells me that the foregoing offers valuable guidelines for choosing where to work. Those of you who heed them will enhance your chances for satisfaction. Those of you who don't will probably end up joining the "I-made-it-but-hate-it" group.


What about life style? If surfing, skiing or sailing are your bag, your locale choice is automatically restricted.

Don't discount the importance of life style. A very successful high-tech engineer I know who had everything going for him in a job he loved began packing his things one day after he realized he simply couldn't continue without weekend sailing, an activity not available less than 100 miles from his then-home.

Before making a career move, review *all* the reasons you would or would *not* be content with a job's location. Too often the grass *does* look greener on the other side of the fence, but do some homework and introspection before leaping over it.

## Economic Factors That Make
## The "Where" Question Important

Besides these lifestyle considerations, you must also face questions of economics. A little research should uncover prevailing pay rates (so you can compare them with what you've been offered), costs-of-living, tax rates, housing costs, etc. in the area or areas you are considering.

You'll find pay scales can differ by more than $5,000 for similar jobs in different places, while living expenses can vary by ten percent or more. While you will know the pay the employer is offering you, you'll want to know about prevailing salaries in the prospective location to determine: (a) whether or not the salary you are being offered is fair and (b) whether switching jobs will mean moving again to get a comparable salary.

The best advice I can offer is the simplest: Ask people you know for help; if necessary, identify friends of friends. If you're thinking about moving to Phoenix, contact someone who lives there. If you can't find anyone, ask Personnel to give you a name or two of employees—if possible, those originally from your home state. Failing that, look for help from organizations to which you belong.

Another reliable source of free advice are chambers of commerce. Local chambers often can supply much information, including names and telephone numbers of agencies that offer specific information on housing and other topics. Some chambers have combined to publish a quarterly "Inter-City Cost of Living Index," giving a comparative cost-of-living figure for 292 cities. It includes food, housing, utilities, transportation and health care, butdoesn't consider taxes.

Another prime source of salary and cost-of-living information is a series of books published by the Compensation Institute, a division of the William M. Mercer Co. of New York. Used primarily by personnel departments, the volumes provide specific cost and salary information for hundreds of places. Check out your public or college library or locate a personnel department that has the set available (since this valuable source costs more than $600).

And don't forget local newspapers, which can help you check the information the chamber or others give you. Newspapers and local magazines can give you the best feel for the food, housing and rental prices in the area.

Your best sources for tax information are independent taxpayer organizations. At least 40 states have such groups, almost always with headquarters in the state capital. Note: The state income tax in various states varies from none to "light" to "exorbitant."

# Are *You* Ready For The *Right* Job?

Choosing the right job is a challenge that deserves your fullest attention. Only by doing so can you hope to become a winner, reach desirable levels of achievement and satisfaction.. and avoid the "I-made-it-but- hate-it" syndrome.

To reinforce the superior effort you will make to select the "right" career, organization and job, experience tells us one final selection will put you in the driver's seat: choosing the "right" boss.

## Are You Ready for The SAT I ...

# 6

---

# CHOOSING THE RIGHT BOSS

---

He treats people like machines.

What a wonderful experience working with him.

He's an unadulterated S.O.B.

He's too nice, doesn't expect enough from his people.

    —Actual quotes from the career world about bosses.

**A**h, the Boss! Who will he or she be? Leader? Tyrant? Coach/Teacher? Friend? Foe? Career booster? Career blocker?

Is it possible for a college graduate to select the *right* boss the first time around? What should you look for, and how can you get the information needed to make a winning decision? How many times do you have to get it wrong to get it right?

No matter how well you've done choosing the right career, organization and job, you may wind up unhappy, disappointed and out of a job if you don't choose the right boss. Experience tells us that, next to marriage, no relationship will be more significant in your adult life than the one with your boss.

## The Boss Connection

You will find in your first 90 days in the job, as the rest of us have, that your relationship with the individual who runs the show plays a pivotal role in the career game. The "becauses" are many. Because a Boss can:

- Explain what's expected of you—or let you play a dangerous guessing game.

- Help you over the rough spots—or let you founder.

- Give you plenty of rope so you can free wheel—or give you plenty of rope so you can hang yourself.

- Offer guidance—or let you drift.

- Give you space, lots of breathing room—or breathe down your neck.

- Share plaudits and other psychic rewards—or take all the credit.

- Make work fun, a satisfying life experience—or demand that you be available day and night, weekdays, weekends, always at his beck and call.

- Accept blame for snafus—or quickly point the accusing finger in your direction.

- Provide opportunity for growth and accomplishment—or restrict your chances, box you in.

- Use power to give you decent raises—or limit or withhold them.

- Use power to promote you—or demote or fire you.

- Treat you like an associate—or constantly remind you you're an underling.

- Let you become a "speaker-upper"—or fit you with a muzzle.

- Treat you like a human being—or demean and bedevil you into an obsequious flunkey.

- Keep you tuned in—or leave you in the dark.

- Serve as a desirable reference when you leave— or kill your chances for landing the next job you want.

- Let you participate in goal-setting—or make you dance to his tune.

In short, your Boss can *boost* your career—or *batter it to a pulp.*

Choose *right,* and you can expect a satisfying relationship, one that will help you to put your career on fast forward. Choose *wrong,* and you will have something in common with Custer.

This chapter's aim is to set your sights on this critical choosing activity and help you to make the right decision. Keep in mind that the definition of the "right" boss will vary greatly among individuals. Some like tough, disciplined demanding bosses; some don't. Some need a supportive supervisor; others couldn't care less. Some can tolerate a tyrant if the money and perks are right, just rolling with the punches; others will be intimidated and suffer psychic and career damage.

Selecting the right boss really boils down to finding the type of leader that suits *you,* the person with whom *you* have the best chance of performing up to your potential.

Granted, it is the subordinate's responsibility, not the boss's, to accommodate, to be flexible, to adapt. Your goal, however, is to select a boss with whom you can enjoy a more "natural" relationship, one in which you can concentrate on *accomplishing,* not spending your valuable time "accommodating," being "flexible," and "adapting."

The first step in this process is to become acquainted with bosses—their types, their styles, their pros, their cons.

# Where Does Your Boss Fit?

Read over the quotations at the beginning of this chapter. They represent the major types of supervisor you will find out there: The Demanding, Do-Or-Die Type; The Resolute-But-Responsive Type; The Laissez Faire Pushover Type.

## The Demanding, Do-Or-Die Type

The first quotation offers more than an adequate clue to this type's "management philosophy." Although in a minority today, they're still out there—Neanderthal tyrants. Often workaholics, though not necessarily, they have great drive, get things done, are likely to work ungodly hours...and will expect you to follow suit.

If such a boss gets to like you (because you grovel after him like an obedient puppy), you've got it made. This kind of boss sees people in strictly black and white terms—there is no room for greys or shadings of any kind. You're either "in" or "out," with him or ag'in him.

Because they are subject to fixations and hang on stubbornly in the face of problems and adversity, such bosses often become stars or superstars. If you dance to their tune and they like you, you can accelerate your career along with theirs.

Of course, there are many problems working with this type, one of which is, as the quotation said, that they can use you, then "chuck you out." So if your personal orientation and makeup allow you to select and, at least temporarily, succeed with such a boss, just keep honing your sense of timing so you're ready to move on to better things before he gets rid of you.

The best example of this type of boss that comes to mind is Roger Templeton (not his real name), a CEO who retained my services as a human resources consultant after experiencing people problems that were beginning to affect his company's efficiency and profits.

One of the first steps I took was to invite myself to his next management staff meeting. There's no better, quicker way to get acquainted—with the big boss, his leadership style, and his key people, than by observing the interaction that develops in the discussion and resolution of management problems.

It wasn't long before a clue emerged. Roger announced a major decision he had made only hours before the meeting. The intentness with which his subordinates listened told me that Roger had not involved any of them in the decision. When he finished his report, Roger's fixed gaze moved from manager to manager until he completed the cycle. Then came a concluding statement I had never heard before or since: "If anyone disagrees with the decision, signify by saying, 'I resign!'."

After the meeting, I asked him with undisguised surprise, "Is that the way *all* your meetings are run?"

With only the slightest trace of a smile he responded, "A group like that has to be reminded regularly who's boss."

This type of boss will rarely be so blatant about his tendency for using and abusing authority and power. Some are so good at hiding their M. O. you won't find out their real identity for some time.

## How About The Workaholic?

If you also are one, you'll be okay selecting one for a boss. If you're not a super dedicated type, vigilance is called for. (You should have a pretty good idea from your college or past work experience whether or not you fall into this class.)

As a group, "workaholics are surprisingly happy," says psychologist Marilyn Machlovitz in her book, Workaholics (Addison-Wesley). "They are doing exactly what they love—work —and they can't seem to get enough of it."

But workaholics can make the lives of those around them miserable. They have lost all ability to keep work in perspective. They think it takes precedence over everything and expect those who work for them to behave the same way.

Of course, not everyone who works hard is a workaholic. Some simply possess a larger-than-average appetite for work but manage to maintain fulfilling personal lives. Many hard workers are ambitious to advance their careers and, either willingly or because they feel pressured in the executive suite, try to fit into the "workaholic executive" mold. The bona fide workaholic, on the other hand, is someone who needs to work *even when no pressing reason exists to do so.*

Your aim should be to identify the boss who is a *hard worker*, because that's the type that makes it to the top...and may take you along with him. But you want to *avoid* workaholics, because they cannot continue to work in the fast lane without creating problems for themselves  and for you...if you agree to hire on.

## The Resolute-But-Responsive Type

Then there are the Good Guys & Gals—the bosses who can make your quest a happy one. There are actually many of them out there, but you have to dig, probe, and evaluate with missionary zeal to make sure you've actually found one.

Do so, and you'll find a Bob Cannon. To most of us who worked with him, he was an inspiration. Before I joined up with Bob, business was simply a necessity for maintaining a pleasant lifestyle. I had forsaken journalism to enter business because of mundane reasons, and accepted as tolerable the necessary actions of routine business which I found somewhat adventureless, bland and humdrum.

Bob changed all that, and also stimulated many brilliant men in our organization. He and his associates built an enthusiastic, results-centered, success-oriented outfit which could be as hard-nosed as a marine drill instructor, but as compassionate as St. Francis.

"Employees," he insisted, "are the key reason our organization has achieved world leadership. Because we have dealt with them on a What's-Right-Not-Whose-Right basis, they have done their best for us."

This type of boss will:

- Be results-centered and expect you to be, too. But he will judge your performance fairly, based on a periodic review of your track record.

- Set high but attainable performance goals and, when possible, set them with your involvement.

- Expect a professional approach to your work, a commitment to excellence. Yet, unlike the Demanding-Do-Or-Die type, he knows there's no such thing as perfection, so you won't have to experience sleepless nights worrying about every mistake you might make.

- Be responsive to your needs as a human being and as a competitor in the success game. He will give recognition when it is merited, make possible financial rewards (also based on merit performance), provide opportunities for achievement and trying the new.

- Expect you to accept personal responsibility for growth in your career and be willing to take on increasingly heavier responsibilities. But he will offer guidance and coaching.

## The Laissez Faire-Pushover Type

The laissez-faire boss is often disarmingly pleasant, so you run the risk of not probing as deeply into his character as you should. "Ah," you are inclined to conclude, "with this person as boss, it's going to be a piece of cake. No pressure. No do-or-die. I'll be able to wallow in a climate of peace and tranquility."

But that tranquil climate more often than not will be minus the sense of urgency that moves individuals and groups toward success—because such a leader has a deep need to be liked, recalcitrants and laggards will not be disciplined to toe the mark.

# Weighing The Chemistry Factor

The success of your interview will hinge on the interaction between you and your potential boss. That interaction—the way you view each other and positively or negatively react to each other during the interview is especially significant for the beginner.

During the interview, size up your prospective boss, especially his reactions to the inquiries you make. The questions I will suggest for your encounter aren't only for the purpose of gaining information. They will also test the all-important "chemistry" level that prevails not only during the employment interview, but also in the first 90 days on the job and beyond.

Chrysler chairman Lee Iacocca, who rescued the big auto maker from bankruptcy, faced a vexing "chemistry" problem when he was with Ford. He called the Fords wealthy snobs who "practiced the divine right of kings. The Fords wouldn't even socialize with you. You could produce money for 'em, but you weren't about to hobnob with 'em."

Henry Ford is widely quoted as having told Iacocca when he fired him that he simply didn't like him.

The key lesson you should take away from this example is that *chemistry is the key factor in the boss-subordinate relationship*. You can have talent, be a peak performer, know all the right moves...but if the chemistry's not "right" with a boss, your quest for a satisfying career may be doomed.

## Five Litmus Questions To Consider During Your Interview

During your interview, you can run a series of five "litmus tests" to determine the chemistry of the potential boss/subordinate relationship:

*Do I receive favorable vibrations—of goodwill, of genuine interest in me as a person and a candidate?*

Or does he make me feel like this is a cat-and-mouse game, with him probing only for weak spots, ready to pounce on any miscues that surface?

*What is my gut level instinct telling me—would we really hit it off or not?*

Would we be likely to accept one another, not be overly critical? Would I be likely to trust this person instinctively?

*Do I get the feeling the other person has a veneer that won't let me get to know him?*

*What are his eyes telling me?*

Open, friendly, inviting a two-way exchange? Or cold, narrowing with suspicion at times, challenging me to react? Is there a steady, penetrating gaze, more like a stare, that says he is getting malignant satisfaction from the role of Inquisitor?

*How is the prospective boss reacting to the questions I ask?*

Welcoming them, conveying impressions such as, "We're talking the same language" or "Your questions are appropriate. You have a sensible approach to your job search?" Or: is he defensive, hesitant, reticent, telling you, "You're off base?"

## How To Handle *Your* Part Of The Interview

Only by developing your own questions, those that will at least give you an inkling as to who your prospective boss is as a person, can you hope to make a decent, reliable choice. Here are questions to ask your potential boss:

*What attributes do you especially look for in subordinates?*

The answer will tell you a lot about your prospective boss and, as a bonus, allow you to compare the expressed expectations with what you have to offer.

*What have you found gets the best results from your people?*

The response should indicate his preference among the three chief options for getting things done—authority, power, or persuasion. How does the response fit with your personal makeup?

### *How many people in your work group have been promoted in the past two years?*

If the numbers are reasonable, it's a safe bet he is a good coach, fosters career growth, provides an environment of success. If few or no promotions have taken place, probe further. Does he hang on to talent, restricting promotional opportunities because turnover creates a "problem?" Were promotions limited because corporate growth had hit a plateau, or could there be some kind of political reason behind it?

### *Since you have been here for some time, no doubt you feel favorably toward the organization. Would you mind sharing with me why?*

Possibly the feedback you get here may reinforce your decision to accept or reject the job. The reasons he offers will tell you a lot about him.

### *What actions on your part have you found best motivate your people?*

Note: In order to diminish the possibility of your prospective boss becoming gun shy at questions like this, you may precede it with a statement such as: "In school we were exposed to some studies on motivation, and I found it especially interesting as it relates to the work situation." Then go ahead with the question.

The prospective boss's answer will probably tell you volumes about his leadership style.

### *What course have you found best for handling an employee who makes a mistake?*

If the answer is, "No one makes a mistake around here and gets away with it," mentally at least you should terminate the interview right then and there. You shouldn't risk your career with a boss like that. Most will tell you, "A mistake's okay, just as long as it's not repeated."

*How often do you and your subordinates get together for a review (preferably planned) of progress, goals, future potential?*

If this review doesn't happen, not even once a year ("Oh, we keep in touch daily"), you'd better think twice. Remember, acceptance (of you and your performance) depends on understanding (on your boss's part), and this can't be achieved unless he is willing to sit down with you *at least* once each year to examine your performance and your potential.

*Hours and work load are no concern in my case. However, I plan to take special night courses, so could you tell me what the average work week is, in terms of hours?*

Note that the question was posed in such a way so it would not give a negative impression. Yet the response can and should lead to further discussion. It will help you determine whether the prospective boss is a workaholic, compare the prospects to who you are and how you feel about the role of work in your life.

*How would you describe the group you supervise?*

If the response is enthusiastic and positive, you have a reliable indicator that this boss may be the one to choose. If the answer is negative—"People today just aren't with it"—be on guard. Wait to see how the wind blows when he answers other questions.

After all, he has the authority to hire or not, so if the employees in question are numskulls, who's the biggest dolt? If "they" aren't enthused and motivated, then most likely the boss is not. How they manage to keep their jobs I don't know, but there are indeed bosses who "demotivate."

# Rating Your Prospective Boss

After your interview, rate your boss-to-be. This checklist will help. Score each trait on a scale from 0 to 10, with 10 being highest.

The Boss I am considering is likely to be:

*Communicative:* He'll probably keep me tuned in, so I can function. He'll let me in on what's really going on; I'll always know how I stand, because he believes in reviewing performance.

*Accessible:* He'll be there when I have a problem. Not an isolationist, he'll be where he's needed. His door will be open.

*Sensible:* He probably will expect me to work hard and get results, but he's aware that work is not all. So he won't take a work-should-also-be-a-hobby stance, won't expect me to work night and day and on weekends, won't make me be always at his beck and call.

*Coaching-oriented:* He'll be willing to share his know-how and offer guidance so I don't fall on my face too often. He'll encourage my growth, make me keep raising my sights.

*Decisive:* He's not likely to keep me on tenterhooks, not likely to procrastinate, then demand I hop to it and fill the gap he created.

*Fair:* He won't play favorites. He'll give me a sporting chance if I play ball with him. Though expecting top performance, he'll be reasonable and patient.

*Committed:* And because *he* is committed, he'll respect and welcome *my* commitment, not mistrust it. He'll expect me to be in high gear, take chances, yet I won't have to be afraid to stick my neck out.

*"We"-oriented:* He'll involve me in plans and goals, not set arbitrary, unreasonable goals. He'll be a team type who'll set a good example, share plaudits and rewards.

*Tough-minded:* Not a weakling, laissez-faire type who can't face up to life's realities, he would provide a disciplined, achievement-oriented work environment, one in which my career could experience vigorous growth.

*Caring:* His friendly demeanor and wholesome views about the people side of management indicate he would care about me as a person, using his status and power to help me achieve personal goals.

How did your potential boss rate? If the total rating is 50 or more, the odds are in your favor. And, obviously, the closer to 100, the better the boss! Accept the job if it is offered. If the rating is less than 50, forget it. Don't let positive thinking bamboozle you. You will be playing against a stacked deck. Play with him and there will be 52 reasons why you won't end up as a winner.

You will note I did *not* suggest that your prospective boss bat a thousand. No one is perfect as a boss. Remember that, and you will get along better with any boss type you choose.

Each preceding chapter has a direct bearing on how well you will do in the first 90 days on the job. Now let's come to grips with the nitty-gritty factors of success and survival in that initial, probationary period of the job you have chosen—the specific smarts, attitudes, action, do's and don'ts that will propel your career in the right direction, giving you a flying start during your first 90 days on your first job or at a new company.

# 7

# THRIVING DURING
# THE FIRST 90 DAYS

The superior beginner discovers upon entering the career world that success and survival happen when you use your best skills, talents, and abilities and apply them toward improvement of the enterprise.

Nervous?

Most people are when they begin a new job. The unfamiliar surroundings and people, the pressure to make the right impression, the desire to prove yourself all over again—no wonder you're exhausted by quitting time!

But you're not the only one who's nervous. Your boss is hoping *he* made the right decision when he chose *you* rather than one of the other promising candidates. You can bet he'll be sizing you up, making sure that you're going to help him look good.

You're on probation. The company might tell you this point blank during the new employee orientation process. But whether they do or not, you can bet your actions will be looked at carefully during your first three months on the job.

While knowing this hardly relieves the pressure, one thought might help you handle the pressure a little better: Your new employer is also on probation. While *you* might have a lot to prove to the organization, *the company* also has a lot to prove to you, just as it did during the interview process. Is the job everything your new boss said it would be? Have there been any unexpected duties foisted upon you? Is your boss's behavior consistent with the way he acted during the interview?

You are not a helpless specimen during the first 90 days on the job, but a participant in a joint venture in which you and the organization are building a future together. You have a great deal to do with the opinions your superior and others in the organization form of you.

This and the following chapters will help you adjust to your new surroundings and help you make the best impression —during the period that counts the most. Recent graduates, as you'll soon see, are most at risk during this period. Much of the first part of this chapter is directed to them.

# What You Don't Know *Can* Hurt You

If you're a brand-new graduate, your expectations of the career world were shaped to a large extent by what you've heard in the classroom. Academia has given you an essentially optimistic view of what will occur and what your new employer will expect of you. This is good. Just remember that the real world seldom lives up to its advance billing.

Most students are taught to see things in broad perspective, to think in terms of general concepts. If you were a business major, you were taught to think as a generalist.

So what usually happens? In the first 90 days on the job you receive a rude awakening. First, you'll probably be given routine tasks to do that have little or nothing to do with the "big picture." And, sometimes directly, often with just a polite nudge, you are given the message: Put the views you had in college into deep freeze.

As a result, many recruits in the critical 90-day period become convinced they've been cut off from the very academic exposure that prompted the organization to hire them in the first place.

You might even agree with the view one graduate expressed to me: "This is a farce. The very education I needed to land this job they now want me to ignore. There are signs all over the place that I'd better do just that if I want to belong and get ahead."

# What Do They Want From You, Anyway?

I have seen this happen again and again: Each year organizations invade college campuses seeking ambitious, talented people. Organization and graduates are delighted with the prospect of working together. Then, too often, and too soon, the romance turns sour .Why?

The young graduate feels the company is stifling him, that he doesn't have a chance to grow fast enough. On the other hand, the organization at times feels it made a mistake hiring another crop of whiz kids who don't whiz.

Why does this situation keep recurring?

It seems especially odd when you consider the fact that the organization's goals and yours seem basically alike:

- The organization expects results. Just out of college, you  will want a chance to show what you can do.

- The organization hopes you will step into a position of responsibility after you have gained some experience. You are intent on building a career in administration or management.

- The company expects a day's work for a day's pay. You want a job you can sink your teeth into, one that challenges your initiative and fills a need for a sense of accomplishment.

- The organization wants to capitalize on up-to-date knowledge you, as a recent graduate, may be bringing from the groves of academia. You want a chance to put into practice what you have learned.

- The organization wants its leaders-to-be to be generalists, to see the "big picture." You want the opportunity to gain broad experience, be exposed to the many facets that make for progress, and to contribute your talents and knowledge.

How compatible can goals get? Sounds like a made-to-order relationship. It should be, but all too often it doesn't turn out that way.

## Sharing The Blame

The fault in most cases is shared:

- The organization drops the ball from the beginning. It does not take steps to assure that the compatibility of goals is preserved.

  During the first 90 days (sometimes it stretches out to a year or so), the organization sees the job as a sink-or-swim test, a "trial" assignment as a non-entity assistant and/or a no-account errand boy who either (a) doesn't receive any training and has to learn catch-as-catch-can; (b) is exposed to superficial, non-relevant training; (c) is exposed to a training program that spoon feeds him/her information

he already had in school; or (d) has the good
fortune (rare) of plunging into a sensible, guided
management-trainee program.

- The recruit gets off on the wrong foot. It's so easy
to do that. You have every right to your expectations. Yet you face a severe test.

What follows are some suggestions for passing that test.
While directed primarily at the new graduate, I think even the
most grizzled veterans will find some applicable advice.

# Putting Your Career In High Gear

The following set of valuable recommendations is from
members of The Personnel and Industrial Relations Association
of Los Angeles. Their views are worth considering, because they
know what line executives want and they have seen firsthand
what behavioral patterns enhance success and which do not.

*Mary Lou Pyle, Vice President-Personnel, Home Savings of
America:*

First impressions *are* lasting! Appearance,
attitude and mien are the primary aspects of evaluation in the first 90 days. Leave your new broom
(you know, the one that "sweeps clean") at home.
Ask, nay, *plead* for help from the old hands. Don't
assume because you've "read the book" you can
conquer all in your first 90 days.

The first three to six months in a new job are
essentially non-productive for you. You must learn
the company, its philosophies, its politics before you
can effectively apply your knowledge. Adopt a neu-
tral philosophy and soak up all the information you
can. When you've got that all together, you will just

be starting to become an accepted, integral part of the operation.

*Norm M. Kellett. Corporate Vice President-Industrial Relations for NI Industries:*

So very much depends on what the new employee expects and what the company expects and is willing to do to accommodate the graduate. Newly-hired graduates tend to have job expectations that are incompatible with job requirements. The result often is psychological and/or physical withdrawal from the job.

The most important suggestion to a newcomer: Don't be afraid to ask questions. Next, be willing to do everything required and then some. Better to be told to slow down than to speed up. Be willing to help whenever practical—don't wait to be asked. Learn your own duties and as much as possible of the other jobs around without incurring disfavor."

*William C. Stoner, Manager Employee Relations and Public Affairs for Procter & Gamble:*

First and foremost, get your employer's expectations straight: What exactly does your organization expect from you—and when. Learn, as soon as possible, your employer's goals and objectives, then make some *early* contributions toward their attainment with your job assignments, regardless of how small they may be in the first 90 days. And: ask a lot of questions!

The new employee should read everything he can get his hands on that relates to his company and his job—starting with the employee handbook.

The newcomer also should observe and seek to understand the relationships among the people with whom and for whom he works—without passing judgment. Be friendly to all, intimate with none during the early days.

New employees should seek to make a contribution as early as possible. Such contributions are usually best made by producing excellent work on assigned tasks. Attempting to effect change in established routines or reorganizing the place can come later, *after* the newcomer is well established and has proven that his opinions are worth listening to. Avoid at all cost the phrases, "When I was in school..." or "At XYZ Company where I used to work they..." I think it boils down to this—"large ears—small mouth."

# Pleasing The Boss

Here are some tips on what bosses like to see in new employees:

- *Keep busy on company work.* If you complete your assignments, ask for additional work or suggest another assignment yourself. Don't spend company time on unnecessary personal phone calls or other private business.

- *Show initiative.* Volunteer for learning opportunities, extra duty, the unwanted task. Make suggestions that will save time and money. Do something extra!

- *Make it a point to get assignments done on or ahead of time.* A reputation for being responsive is like money in the bank!

- *Start early and stay late*—if permissible. Such action will preclude being late and will quickly be noted as a very positive sign.

- *Learn from your mistakes.* Mistakes are inevitable. Simply own up to them and be ready to point out how you will prevent them from recurring. Always be receptive to suggestions on how to improve your performance.

- *Bring alternatives to the boss.* Don't bring problems. Analyze the problem and think through alternate solutions, then present to the boss what you think are the best solutions.

- *Ask questions and take notes.* Your supervisor will automatically assume that you understand if you don't ask questions. So ask away when you need to and don't be afraid of appearing stupid. However, you may appear stupid if you ask the same question twice. Well organized notes will minimize that possibility.

- *Check your understanding of assignments by restating them in your own terms.* Check your assumptions!

- *Check back (only occasionally) to let the boss know how you are progressing,* especially during your first week on the new job.

- *Learn and then comply with the formal rules and informal norms.* Follow the norms of dress. Wait till you have clearly established yourself before coming to work, for example, without a necktie—unless that is clearly the acceptable dress norm. Blend in and don't create unnecessary problems.

- *Be discreet.* Confidential company information such as salaries, employee relation problems, etc., should be *kept* confidential. Divulging such choice morsels may make you popular on the grapevine, but it can be the "kiss of death" if discovered by your supervisor.

- *Learn as much as you can about the company—* its history, organization, products, and policies. Ask your boss what information he feels is important and how it relates to your job and your department.

# Creating Good Relationships With Others

Establishing and maintaining a positive work climate with other employees is important. Some guidelines to consider in the day-to-day contact with other employees are:

- *Be positive, pleasant and upbeat.* Smile a lot, and don't put anyone down. Let the clever cheap shots go by. Stay out of internal office politics, if at all possible.

- *Express complaints as constructive suggestions or questions.* Complainers, particularly new employees, are seldom appreciated and not long tolerated.

- *Don't use off-color language, or tell ethnic or sexist jokes.* What is humorous to some is offensive to others.

- *Avoid continually referring to a former employer,* if you had one. Fellow employees don't like to hear continually about "the way we did it at the XYZ Company." Even though well-intended, such comments wear thin quickly.

- *Participate in office and company activities.* Attending the company picnic and office luncheons gains visibility and shows interest that will eventually pay off.

- *Don't show enthusiastic agreement with any criticism.* If people bend your ear, criticizing peers, bosses, or the establishment, play the psychologist's role—put on your most intent, sympathetic listener's mask and offer no more encouragement than a coldly objective "Hmm" until you've had ample opportunity to size up the critics and the objects of their criticism.

- *Don't offer observations, opinions, or criticism about the generation that preceded yours,* no matter how well deserved. In the first month, don't even do this with "under Thirties." Many people in your generation don't have hang-ups about age. They aren't uptight about elders, so reaction here could detrimentally affect your relationships and your image.

- *Use the Socratic Method.* When you are involved in strategy-type discussions, trying to sell ideas, plans, programs and yes, yourself, don't tell—ask. Ask questions with which the other person would have to agree. Get them to say "yes, yes, yes" and you will not only make/help friends but gain the support you need.

- *Welcome "coaching"* from those who already have stubbed their toes a few times on the achievement road.

# The Importance Of Finding Mentors

You can initiate pleasant and helpful relationships with fellow workers during your first 90 days that can enhance the progress of your career. There are a lot of great people in the working world. The trick is to find them. Get to know the politics of your organization, the organizational structure, and how people fit in.

To get to know the people that can prove helpful to you:

- *Be all ears,* note whose name(s) are mentioned most frequently in positive terms. Who are regarded as high achievers? To whom do others seem to go most often for advice? When you have organizational and/or functional questions, to whom do they refer you (other than your boss, of course). To what people does your *boss* refer you to for reliable information? Make note of those names. Seek those people out to establish rapport.

- *Broaden your network,* touch bases with others outside your group. As a beginner, you are in a good position to do this. Ask your boss and the top personnel executive to help you. This is the fastest way to develop a broad perspective of the company and to find potential mentors. And, if you inquire, you can get from them invaluable views on (a) how others view your group and (b) how your group can be more effective.

- *Don't be satisfied* with the mentoring your boss provides. He may be super, but his efforts will be slower. He has to sandwich in guidance activities between many other priorities.

## Avoiding The Three-Martini Lunch And Other Hazing Tactics

Jim Sweeney, as we shall call him, was a magna cum laude graduate who had been selected by a prestigious blue chip corporation to become one of its management trainees—tantamount in that outfit to wearing an "I Am On My Way" button.

One day he was invited by three fellows from another department to lunch. "Since it's your first, we'll treat," they said.

And treat him they did—lunch, two martinis, and a Drambuie. When they swayed into the office lobby, Jim's boss happened to be there.

Jim was lucky. His boss knew the group delighted in treating fresh graduates to long, liquid luncheons and that the tactic had but one objective—to make the new star rookie look bad.

Far-fetched? It can't happen to you? I have known many Jims. Some were not as lucky as he. Take care. Be cautious.

Here are some tips to keep in mind when you are invited to lunch:

- If the lunch is becoming a two-hour repast, excuse yourself, mumbling something about "that deadline I have to meet" and leave—unless your boss is part of the group, of course.

- Be careful about having cocktails.

- Make sure those who invited you to lunch are not in the organization's Loser's Club. Don't let yourself become part of the wrong crowd in your first month on the job.

## Are You A Morning Or Afternoon Type?

Perhaps your academic experience has already told you which you are. The important thing to do in the first 90 days is to establish clearly whether you are strongly one or the other. Only a few of us can be in high gear A.M. *and* P.M.

To the extent possible, schedule your most difficult and exacting work for your best time of day. This will help you tackle tough problems more successfully, and make better decisions.

# Dressing For Success

People communicate more through their dress than most of them realize.

I vividly recall a dinner party a CEO held at his Beverly Hills home for his top executives. Typically, after the second round of cocktails, the barriers came down. The wife of the sales executive became engaged in a lively discussion with the CEO.

At one point she needled him about her husband's salary level. His retort: "Do you think if I gave him a raise he'd stop looking like an unmade bed?"

The company was experiencing very rapid growth. The sales executive didn't have the opportunity to grow with it.

Months later he was gone. It would, of course, be speculative to assume that the man's dress was a major factor in his termination. However, being close to the picture, knowing his performance level and potential, I am convinced that what he wore and how he wore it was a factor.

## For Men Only

In our world of constantly changing fads and fashions, there still are certain classic, standard elements of the wardrobe that never change. In most situations, you will do well to accept the following suggestions on how to wear you clothes and how to achieve the right fit:

- *Shirt:* Is reasonably crisp (collar and cuffs firm, preferably starched) with no puckering at the seams. Have a large selection of blue, white, and subtly-striped shirts.

- *Shirt cuff:* Extends about one inch beyond sleeve of suit jacket.

- *Jacket collar:* Lies firmly against the neck, with no gaps to one side.

- *Jacket:* Exposes about one inch of shirt collar at back of neck. Jacket left open when vest is worn. Jacket bottom covers seat. Keep top button closed in two button jacket when a vest is not worn.

- *Vest:* Leave bottom button open. Vest should cover belt.

- *Trousers:* Should fit closely to body at crotch and avoid bagginess at knees. Must have sharp crease. Trousers slightly break on shoes.

- *Socks:* Shouldn't show when walking. Colors: blue, black, dark brown, dark grey only.

- *Shoes:* Polished, of course, and not run down at the heels. Should be black with black or blue suits, brown with brown and light grey suits.

- *Belt:* Leather, with simple metal buckle.

- *Tie:* Wide or narrow, depending on the current fashion; knotted firmly, not flat and/or bulky. It should end at the belt buckle, not shorter, not longer.

## For Women Only

Women who want to move up in the organization should heed the following rights and wrongs of dressing for success:

### Right

- Solid, understated colors.

- Coordinated jackets and shirts.

- Darker colors when it is important to convey an image of authority.

- Classic, unpretentious styles.

- Well-tailored dresses that can be worn with a jacket.

- Pumps: quality, medium heeled.

- Blouses, shirts: long-sleeved.

- Jewelry: simple, preferably silver or gold.

### Wrong

- Slacks, knickers, culottes, and such.

- Gaudy, jingly jewelry.

- Flamboyant and bright prints.

- Trendy clothing and accessories.

- See-through and/or low cut blouses.

# The Necessity Of A Performance Review

Most progressive organizations require supervisors to evaluate newcomers' performance and give them an opportunity to offer their views at the end of the probationary period.

When hired, you should request that such a formal review take place immediately after completion of the first month on the job. Doing this you can mesh your evaluation of the organization with your boss's evaluation of you  This will put you in a better position to decide to stay or not.

Unless you have established an unusually satisfactory relationship with your boss, the appraisal discussion can be somewhat stressful—for you *and* the boss.

To help reduce tension and engage in a productive discussion of your performance develop a review from your point of view. You can put yourself more at ease, and gain self confidence by answering the following questions about yourself, your boss and/or co-workers, and the organization and its policies:

1.  Was I dependable—punctual, not absent?
Were my assignments completed on time?
Yes ( )  No ( )

2.  Was the training and/or indoctrination in
this period adequate?
Yes ( )  No ( )

3.  Did I make an effort to develop friends,
establish effective working relationships?
Yes ( )  No ( )

4.  Were my co-workers helpfuland accepting?
Yes ( )  No ( )

5.  Were my co-workers unfriendly, perhaps
hostile, political?
Yes ( )  No ( )

6.  Does the job content match the job described to me before I was hired?
Yes ( )  No ( )

7.  If not initially, does the job offer a chance to use what I learned in school in the near future?
Yes ( )  No ( )

8.  Do my inquiries indicate desirable promotion opportunities from this job?
Yes ( )  No ( )

9.  Has the boss explained my responsibilities clearly, so I know what is expected of me?
Yes ( )  No ( )

10.  Do I feel comfortable with him, know we have a "good" relationship?
Yes ( )  No ( )

11.  Has my experience so far indicated he'd let me free-wheel, use my initiative, not keep the reins tight?
Yes ( )  No ( )

12.  Has he been supportive?
Yes ( )  No ( )

13.  Has he treated me as an associate?
Yes ( )  No ( )

14.  Have I felt able to speak up, offer opinions, suggestions, not felt muzzled?
Yes ( )  No ( )

15.  Has he kept me tuned in, so I know what's going on?
Yes ( )  No ( )

16.  When assignments/goals were set, did he allow my involvement?
Yes ( )  No ( )

17. Is he reasonable in his expectations?
Yes ( )  No ( )

18. Does he ask, rather than demand?
Yes ( )  No ( )

19. Are the organization's policies people-oriented?
Yes ( )  No ( )

20. From what I have seen, heard, experienced so far, will I be proud to tell people where I work, assuming I stay on board?
Yes ( )  No ( )

21. Is there an organized effort to identify who's promotable, and are there development opportunities offered within and outside the organization?
Yes ( )  No ( )

22. Do I like and respect the people who will be my co-workers if I stay?
Yes ( )  No ( )

23. Is there a sound pay and benefits structure based upon a merit review procedure so I will be compensated adequately?
Yes ( )  No ( )

24. Do I believe in the work/products/services of the organization?
Yes ( )  No ( )

25. After the first 90 days am I convinced that politics are not debilitating?
Yes ( )  No ( )

26. Is employee turnover at an acceptable level? Do people seem content to stick with this team?
Yes ( )  No ( )

## What To Do (And Not Do) During Your Review

*Take notes.* Ask if it's okay. If your boss says yes, record any important points covered, especially those concerning follow-up actions and/or what your boss intends to do to help in your development.

*Listen.* Sharpen your listening skills for this session, so you don't miss a single important item. Especially listen for "hidden" meanings.

*Speak up.* Too many bosses are not as skillful with such interviews as they should be. Although ideally you should share equally in the discussion, some people are inclined to monopolize. This is your opportunity to toot your horn and, if you'd like to stay at the company, the *best* time to express your positive attitude about your job and the organization.

*Ask for specifics.* If your boss uses general terms about your performance (positively or negatively), discreetly request examples. Terms like "your communication skills," "your report writing," "your co-worker relationships," or other such general terms are of no value without specific examples. Only specifics will help you to understand your boss's views and help you identify your strengths and weaknesses—and how *he* sees them.

*Avoid criticisms.* Having arrived with a fresh pair of eyes 90 days previously, you can experience a strong temptation to let your boss have both barrels. Avoid the temptation.

*Ask to see the performance review*, especially if you feel uncertain about how the review session went or you feel criticism was offered with which you don't agree. Most companies will offer to let you read that important document and ask you to sign it, attesting that it was discussed with you.

So now you know a little more about how to survive your first 90 days on the job. But winners don't merely *survive* during this all-important period of their careers. They use the first three months on the job to convince their organizations that they *are* winners.

In the next chapter, we'll examine some pragmatic, reliable guidelines from the career world for becoming a valued employee—one who will last far longer than 90 days.

# 8

---

# GETTING OFF TO
# THE FASTEST START...
# WITHOUT FALSE-STARTING

---

The superior new employee approaches each day with awareness, mental antennae in place, keenly alert to a new environment and the people in it, striving to establish identity with the group, its aims, its aspirations. The big question: How best do you do this?

In track and field, there's a thin line between a *false* start and a *fast* start. The same is true of the start you get on a new job.

You will be looking for an edge that will help you be a winner, to dash ahead, be innovative, stand out from the pack.

But, as you've heard many a sportscaster note, success depends more on fundamentals than anything else.

Before you can do well in your race to success, you have to learn (or refresh) two general skills: communication skills and people skills.

Granted, these do not sound as exciting as foreign currency hedging or computer integration. But success in just about any discipline requires mastery of these two areas.

# Becoming An Effective Communicator

As an employee you will work with and through people; your value to the organization will largely depend on how well you communicate. Your effectiveness will depend on how well you get people to "buy into" your ideas, accept your strategies.

This means mastering some basic communications tools: written reports and memos; face-to-face discussions with boss and peers; letters (often reviewed by your supervisor, especially during your probationary period); and speaking in larger meetings, either as a presenter or committee member.

Ask yourself the following questions now. They will help you to determine how well your communication skills stack up:

- Were papers you submitted in college or reports prepared in your last job criticized for clarity, organization, spelling, and grammar? Take a business writing course at the very first opportunity. It could become one of the best developmental decisions you make.

- Are you positive that your grammar is not sloppy? Do you say things such as "her and I" instead of the correct "she and I?" If you aren't sure, you're in deep trouble. Such snafus will not help convince your boss that you're a winner, unless your technical, scientific, or other skills border on the genius level.

- Can you confidently articulate your viewpoints during discussions at work, in school, in social settings? If not, enroll in a speech course or take the very best verbal presentation training available—join Toastmasters International. Most communities of any size have such groups. Join today. You'll be glad you did. I guarantee it.

- Have you decided to join a smaller organization or a large corporation? In a smaller outfit, your verbal skills are more important, because most communication is on a one-on-one basis. It will also be essential for you to be a good listener.

  In a large outfit, the written message takes on special importance Larger organizations usually have complicated policies and procedures, more layers of responsibility and management, more emphasis on reports and meetings, more need to protect your butt (via memos and meetings) because politics play a greater role.

# Becoming People-Oriented

I often observe framed messages on corporate walls that offer clues about the organization's personality. At one of National Medical Enterprises' acute care hospitals, the administrator's office wall has a plaque with a message that demonstrates his awareness of the importance of interpersonal skills:

## A Short Course In Human Relations

The *Six* most important words: "I admit I made a mistake."

The *Five* most important words: "You did a good job."

The *Four* most important words: "What is your opinion?"

The *Three* most important words: "If you please."

The *Two* most important words: "Thank you."

The *One* most important word: "We."

The *Least* important word: "I."

I would suggest you take these phrases to heart. I can guarantee they will help you move beyond a bit player's role.

People smarts rank with communication as a component of your value as an employee. You no doubt are already aware of your people orientation from your experiences on campus and on the job. In addition, the personal inventory in Chapters 1 and 2 will enhance your ability to determine the quality of your people skills.

The following questions will help you better define that part of your Personal Inventory, better determine what your "people orientation" is today, what people challenges you can expect in the first 90 days on the job, and what you should consider doing to improve your skills in this vital area:

## Your Sensitivity Quotient

How sensitive to others are you? You know already that we all have our personal needs and, though they may vary in scope and depth, we all carry an invisible sign around our necks that reads, "I Want To Feel Important!"

How well you keep this in mind will directly affect your relationships. The answers to the following questions should help you determine your sensitivity level:

- Do you like to tell it like it is? Forthrightness is a desirable trait—unless it is mixed with bluntness and tactlessness.

- Do you feel you know "what makes people tick?" What actions and attitudes on your part prompt people to accept you and respect you?

- How do you relate to authority figures? Dig deeply into the past: How have you reacted and how well or badly have your relationships developed with your parents, bosses, profs, coaches, and those who were in positions of leadership in a club, fraternity or sorority, or other campus activity.

## Your Dependability Quotient

How dependable are you? During an employee's first 90 days, organizations will watch this very closely:

- Do you control time, or does it control you? (See Chapter 9 for more on this.)

- Are you always prompt? Usually? Not as often as you'd like to be?

- Have all your reports and special projects been turned in on time? Always? Usually? Not as often as you'd like?

- In your academic years and on the job, have you put forth more effort than required? Enough to establish acceptable grades or reviews? Fallen short?

- If you took part in extracurricular activities during your school years, would your peers rank your dependability as (a) superior? (b) satisfactory? (c) less than satisfactory?

## Your Flexibility Quotient

How well can you adjust to change? Are you ready to roll with the punches? Your initial responsibilities in an entry-level job (often extending a year or two beyond the first 90 days) might be mundane, very routine, unchallenging, not at all related to the exposures academia offered.

The rosy picture painted by a recruiter did not include a warning that entry level jobs too often are yawners. You'll have to be patient and accept these shortcomings so common to first jobs.

Also, nothing in the employment milieu is more challenging than working toward common goals with diverse men and women. Again and again, your flexibility will be tested, because you will deal with many types—caring, uncaring; helpful, indifferent; selfish, unselfish; trustworthy, and not. It often will be difficult to be polite to and respectful of such people, but just as often, you will have to be.

## Learning To Count To 10

Of all the people skills you need, patience is probably the toughest to master. But master it you must.

When you feel your patience has been tested to the limit and you are about to explode, find a quiet place where you can be alone, if that's possible. Step back, take a few deep breaths, and try to put it all in focus.

Losing your cool on the job will certainly not help your career development.

Your superiors will think you're a hothead whose unable to handle pressure.

Your peers and subordinates will fear you're becoming unglued, and, as a result, hesitate to bring up helpful suggestions. If you're really prone to explode, they might try at all costs to avoid working with you.

## And To Mind Your Own Business

Another important lesson is that you should compete with yourself, not others.

Although you cannot escape competitive situations, especially when your job is the same or similar to that of some others, follow the example of high achievers: They concentrate their talents and energies on exceeding their personal previous bests, not on beating competitors.

This assures that you won't be overly concerned about other aspirants' strengths and abilities. And by doing your best and raising your standards regularly, you will become a team player. Others will notice, and be less inclined to "play politics" with you. In fact if someone schemes to scuttle your career, chances are good others will come to your defense.

## Learn How To Disagree

Initially, this means learning how to differentiate between competition and conflict. When it is a matter of disagreeing with a "competitor" in a competitive situation in which you have to take a firm stand, your best approach is to start from a position of objectivity and humility—"I'd like to hear your views," or "Maybe I'm wrong, so let's compare notes."

Experience tells us that such an approach softens opposition, because it helps create open-mindedness.

On the other hand, when "conflict" prevails, an entirely different approach to disagreement is advisable. You're better off, for example, to ask for time for research, if possible—to anticipate what your antagonist's position may be and develop counterpoints.

This helps reduce the chance of embarrassment—loss of face among those who are important in your career.

## Develop Political Smarts

One of the things you should become good at almost immediately is "covering your ass." All high achievers I know have made a fine art of CYA. There are a lot of ways to do so; here are a few:

- Always confirm with a written memo: (a) when you have followed through on a request; (b) when differing opinions may challenge your position at a later date; (c) your answer when someone sends you or your boss a memo criticizing you or your work group.

  But *don't* get involved in a "memo contest." No one wins. When it appears that conflict will continue, try a face-to-face, "let's-clear-the-air" approach.

- Keep all memos your boss sends you. Bosses have memory lapses, too. If a new boss comes on the scene and challenges some action or procedure, you will be in position to "defend" yourself by showing him his predecessor's instructions.

- Keep a copy when you request action by another, especially when a target date is involved that's related to an assignment you must complete.

- When you are asked to develop a controversial approach, obtain as many viewpoints as you can. Include these in the report in objective fashion *before you make your own recommendation.* And don't state "I recommend." Say instead: "A preponderance of evidence and views indicate the best course of action to be..."

- When you see you can't meet a deadline or can't get the information needed to complete a report or a project, protect your butt by informing your boss immediately. Bosses don't like surprises.

Getting along is a skill that can be acquired and developed. You might find the following books helpful: Dale Carnegie's <u>How To Win Friends And Influence People</u> (Simon and Schuster); <u>Communication In The Business Organization,</u> by William Schulz (Prentice-Hall, Inc.); <u>Superior-Subordinate Communication In Management</u> (American Management Association); <u>Games People Play,</u> by Eric Berne, M.D. (Grove Press); <u>Effective Communication On The Job</u> (American Management Association); <u>The Power Of Positive Thinking,</u> by Norman Vincent Peale (Prentice- Hall, Inc.); <u>The Yin & Yang Of Organizations,</u> by Nancy Foy (Morrow).

## Surviving A Merger/Takeover

The skills you need to survive during the chaotic days leading to and following a major restructuring of your company are not unlike those needed when you are a raw recruit. Here are some tips for those who must undergo the trauma of corporate restructuring:

1. *Survivors avoid being mesmerized by the rosy picture painted in the initial phases of the amalgamation.* They know that promises of "no organizational changes," "no layoffs," and "allowing local management to keep control," are usually trumpeted to minimize morale problems, an exodus of personnel, and productivity losses—until the predator is ready to make its move.

Wait to see how the wind blows. Keep your weather eye open. Don't let optimism and positive thoughts push caution aside.

2. *Survivors take a synergistic approach to the merger/ takeover development,* using positives and negatives to shape their attitudes toward the interlopers.

Using positives and negatives in combination helps the survivor to develop an attitude that enhances survival. He recognizes the profound truth expressed by the eminent psychiatrist, Dr. Karl Menninger: "Attitudes are more important than facts."

Using that as a starting point, the merger/takeover survivor observes, identifies any promising, positive aspects of the new environment and, at the same time, sniffs the air, trying to detect any developments that could become hazardous to his career.

3. *Survivors begin snooping immediately,* prying into every hole and corner of the outfit that will dominate the corporate environment. The goal: Determine the kind of organization that's absorbing yours. The list should be a long one, just a few questions deserving of answers:

- Do they care about people? Or is it a kick-them-in-the-teeth type of organization?
- Do they promote and enjoy a teamwork atmosphere? Or is it a dog-eat-dog, political system?
- Do they communicate effectively upward, downward, laterally and keep employees tuned in? Or

do they take a don't-tell-them-any-more-than-we-have-to tack?

- Do they appreciate the value of a holistic approach to work and life? Or do they expect and demand that employees always put the organization first—before family, religion, lifestyle, health?

- Do they have a good record in previous takeovers? Were absorbed employees allowed to continue with reasonable autonomy? Were wholesale lay-offs made? Or did they seize total control and intimidate and demean people in the takeover process?

4. *Survivors learn quickly how to select and use the best probing sources.* They know they need some no-nonsense feedback about the invader's track record, to make the critical decision—stay and adapt or make a quick exit.

They look to some or all of the following sources to get at the truth:

- Former employees of a company swallowed by the same takeover artists.
- Employees of a recently taken over company.
- A newspaper's business editor or reporter.
- Security analysts.

# Showing You Have
# The Right Stuff

Survivors select modes of behavior that will increase survival odds in their favor. Review all the guidelines already presented for succeeding and surviving in the first 90 days under normal conditions, without the presence of an intruding organization. Those guidelines will enhance your survival. Then add the following:

- Develop an I-will-give-the-merger-the-benefit-of-the-doubt stance, at least until the probe or some overt/covert actions tell you to get the hell out.
- Take a crash reading course on the art of politics; try to improve your political skills...fast.
- Work at establishing credibility.
- Try to gear yourself to the new mechanism; conform to the tenets of the new regime.

The gun has sounded, you've gotten a good jump out of the blocks, and you're on your way to that goal—SUCCESS.

Like a runner, you're racing against competitors and the clock. In other words, against *time*. Time management is, along with communication and people skills, one of the most important ingredients to success. Time is the great equalizer. How we use it and manage it makes us different.

So, without further ado, let's talk about Time.

# 9

## KEEPING TIME ON YOUR SIDE

Time. Out of it you have to spin health, pleasure, money, content, respect, and the evolution of your immortal soul. Its right use, its most effective use, is a matter of the highest urgency and of the most thrilling actuality. All depends on that. Your happiness—the elusive prize that you are all clutching for, my friends depends on that.

—Arnold Bennett

"How do you manage to get so much done?"

"Where do you find the time?"

Again and again, achievers are asked these questions by those seeking (and hoping for) a magic formula for success. There is only one answer: Those who succeed don't *find* time. They *control* and *use* the time they have available—the same twenty-four hours per day, no more, no less, everybody else has.

# Your Most Important Capital Asset

The way you *use* time is what makes the difference. People of accomplishment realize how priceless the hours of each day are; they don't let them fritter away; they don't squander them.

## How Arnold Bennett Did It

The great Arnold Bennett, as a poverty-stricken young clerk in a London law office, dreamed of having a successful career as a writer. He took a personal, penetrating inventory of himself and decided he possessed the qualities that career demanded.

But he knew this wasn't enough. Time, he concluded, was at one and the same time his most precious commodity and his greatest obstacle. To reach his goals, he knew that somehow he would have to make time to pursue a writing career while making his living as a clerk.

With rugged determination, he budgeted his hours, disciplining himself to a system of living which permitted no waste of precious time. His time budget made every hour serve his purpose, and it worked beyond his most ambitious dreams. His busy pen turned out piles of stories and articles; his first novel was published; and his struggles as a clerk vanished.

A brilliant and successful career was launched. His was a full life, with time for manifold interests—music, the theatre, painting, reading, friends.

At one point in his career, Bennett decided he would share with others his secret of successful living. He would make people aware of time, urge them to use it for the lasting values of life—for achievement, contentment, success. He wrote his famous How to Live Twenty-Four Hours a Day. Let's consider a message from a man who successfully mobilized time:

"You wake up in the morning and lo! Your purse is magically filled with twenty-four hours of the unmanufactured tissue of the universe of your life! It is yours. It is the most precious of possessions...No one can take it from you. It is unstealable. And no one receives either more or less than you receive...

"If one cannot arrange that an income of twenty-four hours a day shall exactly cover all proper items of expenditure, one does muddle one's whole life indefinitely.

"We never shall have any more time. We have, and we have always had, all the time there is."

Read this classic on self improvement. It provides the inspired answer to one of your most vexing success questions: "How do I conquer time, make of it twenty-four golden hours each and every day?." Bennett and tens of thousands of other competitors have done it. So can you!

# Methods That Keep *You* In Control

Your chances for success at the beginning of your career (and later) will skyrocket if you develop the art of managing time. There are some proven methods that can keep you at the controls.

Of course, you must plan ahead. You have to decide what you're going to do each day, each week, each month—*before* the day, the week, the month starts.

For instance, although my normal office hours begin at 8:00 a.m., I arrive at my office by 7:30. Free from telephone and person-to-person calls, I can review, without interruption, the previous day's activities and design the new day's plan of action.

If some day you run your own business or if you become a corporate executive, you may want to emulate a Super-Chief I know. If at all possible, he saves two days a week free of appointments. This allows him time to review progress on major programs, determine whether they are meeting objectives. In other words, he finds time for planning, thinking and checking. These "free" days are also spent reviewing developments related to his field of interest, so that competitors won't leap past him.

## How To Beat The Clock

Most people are not fully aware of what occupies their time. Make a list of what you do as you do it each day. Make sure that it covers a complete work cycle—each day, every day for a week. If you want to tighten the reins on time, you will do this for two, three, and even four weeks. This will maximize the total picture of your work cycle and leave little to chance.

Once you've done this, you are ready for a three-step action approach which will help you to face the challenges of change, control time, and move ahead to greater achievements:

*Action Step 1*: Develop a simple "Success Activity Chart." Draw four columns down a sheet of paper. Label the first column "Go-Go Importance" and under the title write, "(Absolute Musts)." Label the second column, "Go Importance" and under it write, "(Should-Be-Dones)." Label the third column *"Comme Ci, Comme Ca"* and under it write, "(Importance Questionable—But May Be Of Use)." Label the last column "I Couldn't Care Less!" and under it write, "(Trifling Trivia—Eliminate!)."

Transfer the time items from your basic work cycle list onto the Success Activity Chart. You will be surprised at the perspective that emerges.

*Action Step 2:* Let's develop Success Activity Chart II. Use the same four-column approach. Label column one "Red Hot (Most Urgent—Do Now!)." Column two is "Hot (Urgent—ASAP) —Short Range." Column three is "No Rush (No Urgency)—Long Range;" Column four is "Couldn't Care Less (Forget It; If Time's No Problem, It's For Fritterers)."

Transfer the items from your basic activity chart to Success Activity Chart II. Once again, you will be surprised how, after cold analysis, urgency fades for some items, importance rises for others, and vice-versa.

With both charts completed, you are ready for Step Three.

*Action Step 3:* Now you can create a list of "ideal" activities—those that are truly important, truly urgent. Success Activity Chart III simply lists those matters you have placed in the two left-hand columns of Charts I and II.

Armed with these charts, you can level your guns at time problems that could impede your climb up the ladder.

One thing more before we get on with techniques for controlling the clock. You should add to your "ideal" Career Activity Chart any of those things you should have been doing in the work cycle but couldn't because you didn't find time!

## Sharpening Your Sense Of Time

Only by fully understanding the concept of time are we able to use it to the fullest advantage, accomplish what we want to accomplish, and do the things we must do to move ahead.

Sharpening your sense of time is easily accomplished using these methods:

- Be a clock watcher. Keep your eye on the clock. It has its eye on you.

- Purchase a wristwatch with an alarm feature. Let the alarm ring periodically within your day's work cycle. Try to beat your own deadlines.

- Review your success plans (and progress) each and every week. Don't wait a month or a year.

- Be aware that people underestimate the time involved doing what they *like* to do, over-estimate for those activities they don't like.

- Watch out for "Time Drags" like too many telephone calls and unnecessary meetings.

# Ways To Control Your Environment

For many achievers, a major time problem is interruption by: (a) others who don't know the meaning of time; (b) others who don't care about time; and (c) those who don't care about any one else's time except their own.

Here are a few ways to control your surroundings so they don't steal time from you:

- Inevitably, you'll be involved in meetings. Don't hesitate to set your alarm wristwatch for an agreed-upon adjournment time. The alarm will go off and allow you to say, "Sorry, people, I have another meeting." Needless to say, this is not a recommended approach if you're the junior person at the meeting!

- Always be on time for work and for meetings.

- Don't allow friends at work to "drop in" except in "emergences." Let them know you value time. It's not unreasonable to expect pre-arranged appointments, even when you're a freshman on the job. Most people may grumble at first, but if they're worth their salt, they'll respect you for it.

- If your work will involve many meetings, insist, if you're in a position to do so, on an agenda and a time limit.

## How About Non-Career Time?

Many successful people give "free" or "idle" time no more than passing thought. But you should take the same kind of inventory of your "free" time as you did of your career time, and you will discover that you *have* more free time than you realize and *waste* more, too.

In American business, the more satisfied, happier people at the top seem to share one common characteristic: They have not made their personal lives captive to their jobs.

This observation was corroborated a few years ago by a number of studies made of successful and unsuccessful executives. Results indicated that a characteristic of failing executives was their readiness to sacrifice their personal and family lives to their career lives.

Using "free" time to further career success is all right, but not at the expense of other enriching experiences.

Free time includes waiting and riding time. You can save time for family and other important matters by catching up on reading on a commuter train and during business travel.

Every activity, even resting, takes time; so it all boils down to self-analysis—knowing what your goals are and how much of a hurry you are in.

Sound use of time is based upon hard-headed analysis. But let's not admit there "isn't enough time" for career *and* family or for personal well being! A truly successful person will never admit that.

Artists provide a good example to emulate. They sit in the park or on the train or bus, study the facial expressions and gestures of others. They train themselves to record impressions. The artist, because he loves and knows how to observe life, gets the most out of every moment in time.

Do yourself a favor. If you don't have one already, buy a small notebook. Every truly successful person I know has at least one notebook handy. Top executives, authors, actors, artists, scientists, all have an ever-present notebook to capture and preserve ideas that come in their "free" hours.

## Sixteen More Ways To Save Time

Lord Chesterfield said, "I recommend that you learn to take care of the minutes, for the hours will take care of themselves."

If you take his advice, you'll be surprised at how you can enhance your ability to succeed and survive in the first 90 days and, from that point on, reach desired heights of achievement in your career.

Depending on who you are, what you will do in your career, what your goals are, you may be able to use most of these methods:

- Put vibrant life into lulls.

- Be a compulsive note-taker. If you have a free-wheeling mind, ideas can come at all hours. Usually the best ideas come in the quiet hours, the free hours when the mind is free from everyday pressures.

- Become selfish about your time. Don't let others rob you.

- Keep extracurricular activities in perspective. Golf and tennis are wonderful games. They may even become a part of your job or your career. But they and other activities must be kept in perspective. Sure, you get exercise; you get sunshine and fresh air; and maybe they can sharpen your competitive spirit. But if you love them or similar sports so much that they take too much time, put them in focus.

  Cutting your golf, tennis, jogging or other activity time will save you valuable hours for more important things. Like Fairfax M. Cone, Chairman of the Executive Committee of Foote, Cone and Belding of Chicago, you may end up saying, "not playing golf saves even more time than not talking about it."

- Make the most of commuting time. You'll be lucky if you won't have to drive to work. Commuting via bus, subway, train, you can devote going-to-work-time to thinking and reading.

  If, like many of us, you must to drive to work, keep a note pad handy. When I reach a stop light or the freeway jams up, I jot down any ideas that have flashed through my mind while driving. And consider buying a selection of audio tapes available on career planning and a host of other subjects. Make commuting time a time of learning.

- Try not to live too far from your place of work—especially if you live in a megalopolis like New York, Houston, Los Angeles, or the San Francisco Bay area. I know a man who became sharply aware of time and moved closer to his place of work. Between now and retirement, he figures that he will actually have "saved" more than 2,400 days of driving time.

- Train and make the most of your secretary, if you're lucky enough to have one. Train her or him to answer some of your mail and to fend off "time thieves" in the corporation.

- Use prefabricated letters. Routine letters deserve routine replies—carefully written, with built-in flexibility, they can sound more natural and be more effective than replies made in haste.

- Stay in control. A Los Angeles executive I know goes to his office early every Monday morning. He decides and jots down the ten most important responsibilities (in order of importance) he expects to face that week. At 8:00 a.m., he sets to work on Task No. 1. He rarely finds a serious backlog of problems and claims this has increased his efficiency by at least 30 percent.

- Don't get buried in paperwork. Larry Appley, who for many years was president of the American Management Association, at one point in his career got rid of his desk. "Most desks," he said, "only bury decisions." He also rid himself of files and other records and paperwork. An assistant brought them to him when the need arose.

  Sounds like a crutch, a gimmick, doesn't it? But for him it worked. He was highly successful and led the association to undreamed-of growth. Perhaps later in your career if they offer you a bigger desk you, too, may benefit by saying, "Thanks, but no thanks. Take the one I have!"

- Create a "Do-Later" drawer. No matter what your job, you can control time by creating a "do-later" drawer if you decide a desk is important to your activity. Procrastination, properly handled, can be a virtue.

  You can accomplish at least two objectives: (a) Since "do-later" items don't need immediate attention, you can let them pile up for a week or more and not let these so-so matters infringe on the time you can devote doing big things; and (b) often you'll find that a week or month later, 75 percent of these items don't need or deserve attention anyway.

- Identify *your* best time of day. We all differ physiologically and psychologically. Some of us are fast starters, thinking most clearly in the early hours. Others of us get started only after a number of hours beyond the dawn of a new day. Then schedule the toughest challenges for that time. Instead of time slicing away at you, you'll slice away at it!

- Use the telephone only as a tool. Will your career demand a lot of telephone discussion? To make your calls brief and productive, quickly jot down salient points before dialing. Leave enough space between each major point to jot down developments the phone conversation may present. You will not only have a record, but an action sheet to move ahead. Group calls together, if you can.

- Get yourself a fairly new innovation—a gadget you can buy in novelty shops which makes a telephone-like ring. When you get a long-winded person on the wire who prolongs the conversation long after decisions have been reached, simply wind up the gadget and flick it. "Sorry," you say, "I have to take another call."

The telephone has still another value. If, among your future associates, you find someone who takes an hour to discuss what could be covered in ten minutes or a group you meet with that is so undisciplined that they constantly veer off the track, then arrange with an associate to have him call you at an appointed time—probably when the meeting should end, anyhow. "Sorry," you regretfully say, "but I have another matter that needs attention."

• Have lunch in your office, lab, or other work area twice, maybe three times a week. At lunch hour time pilferers leave; phones stop ringing; no one drops in; that sandwich saves you time to move ahead.

• Tell people how much time you have available for discussions. You must stay in the driver's seat if you want to control the clock.

• The fascimile machine (FAX) can be another time-saving weapon. But remember: There is *no* substitute for voice (telephone) or person-to-person communication.

New York radio sportscaster Art Rust Jr. signs off every night with this: "Yesterday is a cancelled check. Tomorrow is a promissory note. You only have today, so spend it wisely."

Indeed, time is the one currency that all people are given in equal supply daily. Don't let it slip through *your* fingers.

# 10

## HOW ACADEMIA SHORTCHANGED YOU

There are obviously two educations. One should teach us how to make a living, the other how to live.

—John Truslow Adams

Is the college experience worth it?

"Of course!" respond the graduates who have already stepped into the career world.

But in the next breath, they will also tell you they often have wondered why college did not prepare them for the "real world."

# Something Familiar—A Quiz!

If you are still in college, the following quiz might help you decide today whether or not college is preparing you to make a living. Most important, it will prompt you to take action *now* to fill the voids academia may be leaving, so you can put your career in high gear during the first 90 days on the job.

Answer each question with one response: an unqualified YES, NOT CERTAIN, or an unqualified NO.

1. Do you feel your current and future academic experiences will help you choose the right career and job, the right organization, the right boss, so you won't experience severe disappointment—or worse—in the first 90 days on the job and beyond?

2. First impressions are important. Do you expect that your college experience will help you develop a potent AGM (Attention-Getting-Mechanism) for the job world? Will it provide you with specific do's and don'ts for your first days on the job?

3. If you are considering entrepreneurship, has academia provided adequate guidance for making the big decision and helped you determine if you have what it takes to make it?

4. Is academia helping to identify what uncertainties, concerns and anxieties you might face when you start your career and learn what you can do about them?

5. Is academia providing exposures that will help you function in your chosen field?

6. What assistance have you had, or do you expect to get before graduation, to enable you to develop an organized, reliable Personal Inventory, a self assessment that clearly identifies your

strengths, areas needing improvement, true interests and talents, so you can feel confident that you're headed in the right direction?

7. Has academia helped you develop the special communication skills needed to achieve success in your chosen career?

8. Do you know enough about stress management to keep the inevitable pressures of a new job from making you freeze at the wheel?

9. Are you prepared for the political and competitive pressures of the job world? Will you recognize the games your peers are playing and do you know the rules?

10. Do you have a strong sense of what it will be like to work in your chosen career?

Give yourself 3 points for each unqualified YES, 2 for each Uncertain, 1 for each NO. Add up your score.

If you scored 24 or more points: Congratulations! You are among the lucky few whom academia is helping avoid career pitfalls.

If you scored 17—23 Points: You are among the majority. Study this chapter as you would for a final college exam. It can strengthen your chances for success and reduce your vulnerability.

If you scored 10—16 Points: You are among those who are being grossly shortchanged by college. You're off to a precarious start, but it's not too late. This book can help you be prepared to begin your career despite the shortcomings of your education.

# Experience Is Too Hard A Teacher

Unlike college, the business world does not consider test scores important measures of worth. Those in charge of achieving results in the real world are more impressed by the success aspirant's commitment, the ability to communicate effectively, the interpersonal skills that help make teamwork possible.

What preparation is academia providing that will help you function as a valued employee? Some say experience is the best teacher, but it is also a hard teacher—it gives the test first; the lesson, afterwards. This often results in some pretty traumatic results for someone who must learn to function the hard way.

Marie's experience offers food for thought. Graduated with honors as a Personnel Management major, Marie had been exposed to the usual basic subjects, with some special courses in organizational behavior, communications, and such.

In her first assignment with a small electronics organization, she found it difficult to function as a personnel administrator. She was shocked in her first 90 days on the job to learn that executives were circling around established company policies, challenging her to confrontation.

She found her knowledge of organization development theory practically useless in helping her fulfill her major responsibility—helping management develop an enthusiastic, results-centered work force .

Each day she saw political infighting swirl about her, some of it threatening to encircle Personnel, which should have been a non-aligned service group. Each day, it seemed, she was confronted with problems academia never warned her about, such as dealing with the employee suspected of being under the influence of drugs in the hazardous die-cast department,.

Some will say, "Well, that's the real world. You must expect those things to happen." Perhaps, but what Marie could have used more than platitudes was good advice on handling stress and dealing with internal politics.

Marie, along with most others with Personnel Management majors, was misled into believing that her role would have to do mostly with the employment process, wage-salary administration, training, etc.

What *could* academia have done for Marie? It should have exposed her to the body of knowledge that helps graduates choose the "right" job, organization, and boss.

At least one of Marie's courses, let's say the one dealing with organizational behavior, should have included a two-week experience in an unstructured encounter group. This is one of the most efficient ways available to learn who you really are and why others do or do not respond to you, why people have difficulty with communication, why people want to be heard, and why and how they compete for leadership.

## People Skills Matter Most

Experience and validated studies indicate that the single most important factor affecting success and failure is the ability to work effectively with others. This includes the ability to understand people and communicate with them effectively.

Jon T. Weakly, National Personnel Manager of Toyota, USA, Inc., told me, "College should incorporate into the curriculum substantial career planning exposures and organizational development tools and techniques, including self-assessment and team building."

If there is a single negative reaction voiced most about college graduates by personnel management professionals, it is the weakness of communication skills.

Lawrence R. Littrell, Corporate Director of Industrial Relations, Northrop Corporation, notes, "Greater emphasis on communication courses is needed--English, both written and spoken, including but not limited to making effective presentations and the use of visual aids."

## The 7 Dangerous Career Myths Academia Should Have Dispelled

Nothing is worse than stepping into a dangerous situation unprepared. Yes, you *may* survive, but *prepared* survival is better than *mere* survival. Here are some career myths that are found throughout the hallowed halls of academia.

## Career Myth #1: "With diploma in hand I can now say, 'I'm prepared.'"

As a current (or almost) graduate, you probably will be more knowledgeable and better prepared for the rigors of the success game than your predecessors. If you are attending the "right" school, you are having an enviable exposure to the latest in "What's New."

But there's so much you don't know about getting around in your career, you have absolutely no reason to be cocky.

## Career Myth #2: "Making it will be a breeze! In short order, I should be able to write my own ticket."

While you should be positive and self-confident, pressing too hard too soon for "writing your own ticket" can put your career on slippery ground.

## Career Myth #3: This being the age of specialization, I should pursue a specialized course of study.

This is true enough—if your aim is confined to becoming a peak performer in your specialty. Being trained as a specialist will, in many instances, have its advantages, especially in early career years.

However, over the long haul, specialization can limit your chances of moving up into management, where the skills of a generalist are required. That's why many people already well into their careers take post-graduate and extension courses to broaden their horizons.

## Career Myth #4: "With diploma in hand, I can wave goodby forever to the tedious classroom grind! "

Not so. The information explosion taking place today, which will only continue accelerating in the '90s, will make "keeping up" tougher. You must respond to the challenge of knowledge obsolescence.

## Career Myth #5: Idealists should choose careers in government or social work.

Perhaps—and perhaps not. If you are social service-minded, investigate business and industry. It needs people like you. You will be amazed at the many opportunities for community service in the business world that will offer greater chances for broader results than in non-business settings.

## Career Myth #6: The name of the game hasn't changed: It's still who you know that counts.

To deny that this is paramount in some situations and organizations is to deny reality. However, in *most* career situations, it's not *who* you know but *what* you know and *how effectively you use it* that will help you move ahead.

In fact, if you do happen to land a job or a desired promotion because of a "benefactor's influence," you will need great skills to neutralize the antagonism of others and preserve the working relationships that, in the long run, count the most in your career.

## Career Myth #7: Leaders are made, not born.

Don't you believe this—the biggest, most pervasive myth of all. If sometime in the future you aspire to a position of leadership, avoid accepting hook, line and sinker what some overzealous positive thinkers proclaim: that you can become whatever you want to be. Listen instead to feet-on-the-ground champions of positive thinking who proclaim that you can become whatever you want to be, but *only* by using to the optimum your given talents.

You should, therefore, determine A.S.A.P. whether or not you have the innate essentials that leadership demands. And if you have bonafide, innate abilities to lead, seek ways to improve your skills—extracurricular activities, student politics, etc.

If you decide leadership is not your bag, accept that fact of life and you will take a giant step toward: (a) Avoiding a blind alley career route and unnecessary failure; (b) Avoiding waste of precious career time; (c) Maximizing your chances for a non-leadership career as a staff specialist or in a similar capacity—one filled with excitement and satisfaction.

Remember: There are zillions of career activities in which you, too, can become a peak performer and a contributing member of society. If destiny or fate or genes or your "karma" points away from the leader's role, so what? Concentrate on a non-leader career path. It's the surest thing you can do to enter the winner's circle.

## Putting It All In Focus

I hope this unflattering look at the career preparation you receive in college will help you realize areas you must learn more about to succeed.

Give it some powerful thought and on Commencement Day, you will step into the real world confident that you are better prepared to handle a career path that leads to a life of satisfaction.

# 11

## CUSHIONING THE STUDENT SHOCK SYNDROME

In Chinese, the pictogram for *crisis* is identical to the one for *opportunity*.

Webster defines "crisis" as a "...turning point, ...a crucial time..."

Both definitions are appropriate to this stage of your life, the time when you are leaving the cocoon of academia to face the real world of a career. And, as these definitions suggest, your attitude toward crisis can have a great deal to do with your success or failure in handling this crucial transition.

The first 90 days on your *first* job represent a big change in your life. Seemingly without warning, Commencement Day will find you ejected from a reasonably comfortable, nicely structured life—classes at clockwork intervals; homework; intramural activities; beer busts; sports. And, depending on your personal situation, no big economic distractions.

You also have the comfort of being part of one big group—the college—and smaller groups that satisfied your human need for "belonging." Maybe you were even a "somebody" on campus.

Suddenly, all that will be gone. You will begin at the anonymous bottom. A Freshman once again. You will face the Unknown, surrounded much of the time by strangers.

You will doubt yourself as never before: "Did I select the right career/job"? "What if I fail, disappoint my family and friends?" "Suppose I make it but hate it." "I'm already feeling stress. What's going to happen when I have to compete and please a boss?" "If I need help, support, encouragement, to whom will I turn?"

Add it all up and it's little wonder that Student Shock Syndrome smothers some people before and after graduation.

If you are beginning to feel anxiety about facing the real world, you are certainly not alone. Take a look at these grim statistics:

- Psychotherapists at the University of Michigan have been treating 10 percent more students every year for the past three years.

- Cornell University's counseling case load has jumped 12 percent a year in each of the past five years.

- The career choice question and the lack of adequate career guidance in academia have brought about a tremendous increase in the number of changes in choices of major. At UCLA alone, 4,737 changes were made in one year.

## Oh No! Do You Have It?

Many changes in behavior and outlook are signs that can clue you into the fact that the Syndrome might develop into a problem for you. These can vary in content and degree. You must learn to identify them. Only by doing so can you take the first step toward a solution:

- You used to look forward to each day. In college, at least some of your classes were an adventure. But these days, even getting up in the morning takes willpower. You feel anxious, perhaps overwhelmed by what's ahead.

- You used to enjoy people—classmates, faculty, relatives, friends. Now you dread the day you'll be going out to that world where people can wield power over your career chances.

- You used to enjoy competition. Now anxiety grips your spirit, because you've heard how often competition can become confrontation.

- You used to feel self-confident, ready to tackle anything. Now you freeze at the very thought of facing the rocky road ahead, because you feel unprepared

## Who The Syndrome Touches

The Syndrome cuts across all social, economic and cultural lines, so if you have it, take comfort in knowing you have lots of company.

Student Shock Syndrome has been receiving much more attention recently in psychological circles and among career guidance professionals, as a very real pre- and post-graduation stress disorder, one that can have varying levels of trauma.

Daniel J. Levinson, Professor of Psychology at Yale University, and author of The Seasons of a Man's Life, calls the 17-to-23 age span the Early Adult Transition, in which young adults straddle two worlds—adolescence and adulthood.

This is the time when the Student Shock Syndrome can develop, because of the breaking away from the security of home and taking the first tentative steps toward independence.

And it can happen to anyone, not, as some attest, only to lifelong neurotics. Mary Anne Rust, a highly regarded psychologist from Encino, California, says, "The Student Shock Syndrome strikes sensitive, psychologically well-adjusted students who are not neurotic or particularly emotionally disturbed."

Why shouldn't we want to retreat into the sanctuary of our own backyard, especially if it's been a place of love and good will?

What's wrong with preferring the familiar stamping ground, avoiding the uncertain? You don't have to worry about rent, food, clothes. No vexing concern about comfort, survival or the future.

But there is good news about the Student Shock Syndrome.

Human beings have unbelievable powers for facing and dealing with problems. What you need to do now is to tap those powers, put the Syndrome in its place, and begin doing it *before you graduate*.

Courage, said Mark Twain, is resistance to fear, mastery of fear—not absence of fear.

## Finding Solutions To The Syndrome

The best way to get something done, someone once said, is to begin. So, begin by coming to grips with the Syndrome, if there is any aspect of it, no matter how slight, that appears to have entered your circumstances.

Then identify your specific concerns. Uneasy about your career choice? About selecting a "decent" organization when the time comes? Selecting a job that excites you? Are you racked by fear of failure? Of success? Is there a vexing tendency to procrastinate, to avoid the unknown?

If you face the Syndrome, don't feel you must go it alone—seek help if you need it. If you feel incredibly apprehensive about starting your career, call a professional who specializes in helping students cope.

# The Self-Esteem Challenge

When Shirley MacLaine accepted an Oscar she proclaimed to the Academy Award audience and millions of television viewers: "I deserve it!" The next day, some of her friends expressed shock. "What an ego!" they cried.

Nonsense. Shirley was expressing well-deserved self-esteem. For years she had worked hard to achieve the film industry's most prestigious award. She had sacrificed. She had consciously worked at self-actualization. She long ago had made a commitment to strive to be the best she could be.

And because she had accepted responsibility for becoming a peak performer, she earned the Oscar. She has every right to say "I deserve it!"

And you do, too!

In fact, lack of self-esteem can lead to undesirable consequences. Dr. Nathaniel Brandon, author of The Psychology of Self-Esteem and Honoring the Self, says, "I cannot think of a simple psychological problem—from anxiety to depression, to fear of intimacy or of success, to alcoholism or drug abuse, to suicide and crimes of violence—that is not traceable to the problem of a poor self-concept."

## Barksdale Self-Esteem Evaluation

Before going any further, take a few minutes to evaluate your self-esteem using the following questionnaire.

Score as follows (each score shows *how* true each statement is true for you):

> 0—Not at all true for me
>
> 1—Somewhat true or true only part of the time
>
> 2—Fairly true or true about half the time
>
> 3—Mainly true or true most of the time
>
> 4—True all the time

1. I don't feel anyone else is better than I am.
2. I am free of shame, blame and guilt.
3. I am a happy, carefree person.
4. I have no need to prove I am as good as or better than others.
5. I do not have a strong need for people to pay attention to me or like what I do.
6. Losing does not upset me or make me feel inferior to others.
7. I feel warm and friendly toward myself.
8. I do not feel others are better than I am because they can do things better, have more money, or are more popular.
9. I am at ease with strangers and make friends easily.
10. I speak up for my own ideas, likes and dislikes.
11. I am not hurt by others' opinions or attitudes.
12. I do not need praise to feel good about myself.
13. I feel good about others' good luck and winning.
14. I do not find fault with my family, friends or others.
15. I do not feel I must always please others.
16. I am open and honest and not afraid of letting people see my real self.
17. I am friendly, thoughtful and generous toward others.
18. I do not blame others for my problems and mistakes.
19. I enjoy being alone with myself.
20. I accept compliments and gifts without feeling uncomfortable or needing to give something in return.

21. I admit my mistakes and defeats without feeling ashamed.
22. I feel no need to defend what I think, say or do.
23. I do not need others to agree with me or tell me I'm right.
24. I do not brag about myself, what I have done, or what my family has or does.
25. I do not feel "put down" when criticized by my friends or others.

To find your own Self-Esteem Index, simply add all scores. The possible range of your Self-Esteem Index is from 1 to 100. Research shows that an SEI under the mid-80s indicates a slight handicap to one's emotional well-being. An SEI of 75 or less indicates a serious handicap. An SEI of 50 or less indicates a really crippling lack of self-esteem—one that handicaps you in all areas and keeps you from "feeling good," especially from being loved and loving.

(The Index is published by the Barksdale Foundation, P. O. Box 187, Idyllwild, CA 92349. It is reprinted here with written authorization of the copyright holder, Lilburn S. Barksdale.)

## Increasing Your Self-Esteem

Boosting your self-esteem is really just a matter of programming your attitudes about yourself. Keep telling yourself: "I deserve it!" Write down all the accomplishments you can recall, minor or major, starting with the latest: your involvement in a demanding activity on campus that will lead to a diploma—tangible evidence of dedication, sacrifice and achievement.

In developing this list, refresh your memory by reading the results of your Personal Inventory (Chapters 1 and 2) Then compare yourself to the traits and talents of peak performers. You will be surprised by the results. When you finish, you will proclaim, "I deserve it!"

Keep asking yourself: Isn't it right for me to seek a life of accomplishments, one that will provide rich spiritual and material rewards? To seek a satisfying career in which I can find people I can respect?

Take some cues from Barksdale. Look at those answers that affected your score adversely, ask yourself why you feel that way, and see if you can change it.

# The Procrastination Problem

Okay, it's confession time. Has procrastination been a problem for you? Are you suffering from it now as you face the prospect of a new life?If procrastination has already caused you many late nights around term paper due dates, it undoubtedly will contribute to the Student Shock Syndrome unless you get it under control. As Arthur Godfrey said, "Even if you're on the right track—you'll get run over if you just sit there."

Drs. Albert Ellis and William Knaus, psychologists who have done therapeutic work with procrastinators, estimate that 95 percent of college-educated people procrastinate. So the odds are that procrastination is one concern that you should not put off thinking about.

Jeffrey Nelligan, while a senior at Williams College in Williamstown, Mass., articulated his procrastination dilemma:

> One gloomy afternoon last fall, I was lounging in a chair at my desk, my mind wandering  Then, from out of nowhere, came a mental thunderclap: Oh my God, in seven months I have to cope with the real world!

> I sat upright. It can't be true. I'm not grown up enough. Dad pays for my meals, a janitor cleans my bathroom, and Mom balances my checkbook. I can't be grown up. I can't even iron.

> College lies in that netherworld between the carefree and the committed. When hearing that I

was majoring in Romance languages, Dad laughed weakly and then talked about opportunities in the burgeoning computer-programming industry   I worked hard and did well in college. But this difficulty with growing up persisted.

My senior year became increasingly clouded with uncertainty. I wasn't pre-law, pre-med, business-oriented, or even a marketable athlete. I was not even sure I was mature.

I tried to accept the idea that the parchment that I'd receive at Commencement would end my journey as a practicing scholar and open wide the educational curtains on the sober reality of job-hunting—three-piece suits, grocery shopping, and apartment living—known by practitioners as the Real World. The whole scenario had me fearing for my sanity.

The maturity with which Jeffrey examined his procrastination concerns, his assessment of the here and now and of the future, predicts that he will do just fine when he faces the final step, the one that precedes entry into our real world. That kind of self-assessment can offer many rewards.

Incredibly, his procrastination story took on a magical twist. His tongue-in-cheek autobiographical sketch added whimsically:

Fate picked that moment to rescue me. One of the numerous scholarships, grants and handouts that I had taken a stab at had paid off. I was awarded a Fulbright scholarship for two years graduate study in Korea. I was free!

Most of you facing graduation day can't expect a Fulbright "gift" to "rescue" you. So let's take a good look at procrastination, try to understand it, and see what can be done to put it in its place, because we cannot pigeonhole career and life plans.

## What You Should Know About It— Before It's Too Late

People make jokes about it but procrastination is really no laughing matter.

Most clinicians and scholars strongly dispute the popular misconception that procrastinators are lazy. They aver that postponement and avoidance of action emerge from a number of causes.

Chief among them is a resistance to authority/control/ leadership. Some people feel comfortable only when they're in control, often experiencing an inordinately strong need to protect selfhood in face of expectations, demands, and evaluation/criticism from an authority figure—professor, parent, boss.

This trait can be one of the toughest you'll have to look in the eye, not only as a cause of procrastination, but as a potential obstacle to success in your career.

If you share it, ask yourself these questions: Why do I tend to resist authority? What can I do about it? Why do I have this strong need to protect my selfhood? What can I do about it?

Good news: You *can* lick this problem. All peak performers I know who have admitted to possessing this procrastination characteristic have also told me that they have licked it.

# Do You Fear Success?

Many soon-to-be graduates are concerned, even ambivalent about success. They fear "making-it-then-hating-it," becoming alienated from friends and family members.

Such anxieties are inextricably bound to the troubling uncertainties of change: Do I really want what comes with success? What will I have to give up to attain success? Will I be able to handle success? (Almost daily we hear about people whose lives are shattered though they climbed to the top.)

Some hard thinking can help solve this problem. If *you* are experiencing any of these concerns, review again your personal inventory, re-assess your goals, re-establish your priorities. Nail down, if you can, at least tentatively, what you really want, what you don't want.

In doing this, identify as clearly as you can your own definition of "success."

Contact people who have become achievers in your chosen career activity. Ask them about their experiences, their satisfactions, their dissatisfactions. Compare these to *your* definition of success. This should give you enough to go on to decide if success is for you.

## Are You Afraid of Failing?

This dread can complicate one's life a dozen ways, not just as a cause of procrastination. If it's not put in its place, it can plague you for the rest of your life.

People who experience this fear seem to have one thing in common: They are perfectionists or would-be perfectionists, who fear they will never be able to achieve standards of performance they set for themselves. They also fear they will not be able to live up to the expectations of others—parents, friends, peers.

If you suffer from fear of failure, admit that you have it and, once you have, try to determine its causes. For instance, Jim Klein (not his real name), when he graduated from a Midwest university (he was an academic All-American football star), was determined to make it big in the shortest possible time.

Jim's aspirations were fueled in part by his admiration of George Allen, who at one time served as coach of the Los Angeles Rams and, later, the Washington Redskins, among other pro and college football teams. Allen was once quoted as saying, "The winner is the only individual who is truly alive. I've said this to our ball club. Every time you win, you're reborn; when you lose, you die a little."

Three months after accepting a job offer with a fast-track electronic firm, Jim's goal of creating a victorious career with breathtaking speed was rudely interrupted. An unreasonable, demeaning boss vilified and belittled him in a staff meeting. Jim confronted the Neanderthal after the session. Jim's quick exit followed.

Jim, the dedicated "winner," felt diminished, reduced to a loser's role when the door was slammed on his embryonic career. He did indeed "die" in Allen's terms, and not just a little.

He experienced severe depression and came to the West Coast, as so many have done, hoping that Southern California, much publicized as Paradise, would shake him out of his distressed state of mind.

However, two months of an unsuccessful job search left him disillusioned.

A fellow alumni who observed Jim's plight—the nearly extinguished competitive spirit and the shoulders bowed down by hopelessness—convinced him to see me for career counseling.

The first thing we talked about was the fallaciousness of George Allen's view of "winning." Long-term success is not based on winning all the time; the individual who has to win every combat is asking the impossible of himself and others and runs the risk of falling on his face the first time he tastes defeat.

The essence of success in today's career world is the willingness to face and accept "downers" as part of the territory and the ability to cope with life's often unpredictable demands.

"The world is a disorderly and dangerous place and always has been. And the man of power must learn to live in it comfortably," observed Michael Korda, in his Power, a valuable book you should add to your career library.

Jim read the book, underlining many passages for future reference. He and I spoke about how only by recognizing failure as a fact of life can one hope to put it in proper focus, defying it to take control. I gave Jim this advice:

- Achievers use failure to bring out the best they have to offer.

- Successful people agree that failure is a far better teacher than success.

- Experience says that bad times, not good times, make for strength.

- It's okay to fear failure. But remember that winners accept adverse experiences as a part of life. They learn to expect them, meet them, use them to build lives of achievement.

Jim and I held long discussions on these truths. Later, he went on a "retreat" to do some hard thinking. He faced his "must-win" complex, courageously inventoried his psyche, and admitted that a fear of failure, more than his "I-want-to-win" attitude, was the negative agent with which he had to wrestle.

Jim won the match. Today he is a top executive at a prestigious Southern California aerospace organization.

## Or Are You Afraid Of *Falling*

Bill Burton (not his real name) is a fast track, very successful New York corporate executive, lives in an affluent Connecticut suburb, and has three children who attended various colleges.

But he is apprehensive about his children's future: "I'm delighted that I was able to afford the staggering education costs, but I'm deeply concerned. I'm afraid they won't find the opportunities my generation had. Today it's going to be more difficult to make a good beginning and to move into a chosen career position."

Bill is in his fifties and most others would probably conclude that his offspring have done fairly well. However, none of his children feel they have been able to achieve their expectations.

A daughter with a Bachelor of Arts degree has been unable to launch a satisfying career and has gone back to school for an MBA degree. One of the sons moved up into middle management in purchasing, but feels stymied, unable to move up the corporate ladder. The second son, with teaching credentials, had to settle for a job in the computer industry; though he has progressed well, both promotion- and pay-wise, he shows indications of becoming an "I-made-it-but-hate-it" victim.

A growing number of similar experiences of children of upper middle class families seem to indicate that the American Dream has become more elusive.

As one graduate told me, "Many of my friends feel as I do—most of us are going to find it tough to make it the way we want to."

Parents share this apprehension. Surveys by the research firm of Yankelovich, Skelly and White found that 64 percent of Americans believe "We can no longer take it for granted that our children will do better." A whopping 80 percent, disdaining the hoopla about the fast-track Yuppies of the '80s, view the 1990s and beyond as a time when everyone will make "downward changes in the way we live."

Discontent about "downward mobility" is understandable. However, its existence is a given, so don't allow self-pity to hold sway. Don't become frustrated. Instead, concentrate on the "controllables":

- Assess what you can do to become a peak performer.

- Ignore what your parents' circumstances were. Look ahead. Be the architect of your future.

- Remember: The past always looks better than it actually was. Accept Charles F. Kettering's advice: "My interest is in the future because I am going to spend the rest of my life there."

# The Bachelor Of Arts Dilemma

Liberal Arts graduates are clearly worse off usually than just about all others in terms of the job search and a successful career start.

Opportunities for liberal arts graduates have shrunk—and will *continue* to shrink—according to Harvard economist Richard Treeman, who says, "The industries that have employed them haven't grown very much—school teaching, federal government jobs." He also notes that if you look at their real starting pay, a very substantial decline has occurred.

Generally speaking, employers are still looking for "career-oriented" degrees, not recognizing the potential and values of a "broad" education. With competition increasing, they are less inclined to consider B.A. grads for downward mobility jobs (secretary, etc.). Since they are already wary of hiring persons who seem over-qualified, they prefer to give more consideration to the career-type degree.

So what do *you* do if you have or are heading for a B. A. degree?

- Don't be discouraged if you find yourself having to consider a "downward" job. Many graduates begin with "downgraded" positions and zoom into fast-track careers within a very few years.

- Rewrite your resume, downplaying achievements, emphasizing your willingness to start at the bottom in a hands-on job situation. Once you have established yourself as a doer, as a results-getter, you can always communicate the well-earned credentials you kept out of your application and hiring interview.

- Prepare yourself mentally *before* graduation: If the job hunt and/or career-start reaches the gruesome stage, consider taking career-oriented graduate courses. After just one semester, you will be able to show interviewers evidence that, at least in part, may erase their shortsighted view of your liberal arts credentials. If you have the wherewithal to continue, don't let all that talk about a glut of MBAs deter you from getting your degree.

- Sharpen your job hunting and choosing skills each summer. Don't spend time on the beach or vacationing with your family.

# Help Is Available

If the suggestions for dealing with the Syndrome outlined in this chapter do not help, you may find personal, psychological counseling—not just career counseling—invaluable, even necessary.

Please note before selecting a counselor that you are not taking that option just to pull you out of the Student Shock quagmire. You are going to get help—for personal growth, for crystallizing your view of self, of others, of options, so you can move into the most important phase of your life.

A wide range of opportunities is available for help. However, unless your situation is terribly desperate, the Syndrome lends itself best to two options: 1. A psychologist who, at least in part, specializes in student problems. Or 2. Short term therapy, the crisis intervention kind, which helps people weather times of special or extreme stress.

My friend, a top corporate executive, was visibly agitated when he told me about his son. "Tom hasn't been sleeping well. He's beginning to isolate himself, goes to his room hours on end. Ever since he's completed college, he's like a different person— no enthusiasm, no sign of the spark he had as an undergraduate. After three weeks of job hunting, he seems to have given up."

When I saw Tom Edwards (not his real name), he was quite open about his problem: "Since the first semester of my senior year, I've dreaded finishing school. At first it was occasionally, but today I'm scared to death about going out into that jungle."

Tom told me he was afraid he'd fail, how he feared disappointing his parents, acknowledged "pillars" in the Wisconsin community in which they lived.

Tom took my advice. He went to a psychotherapist who specialized in short-term therapy (which can vary in length from 8 to 20 weeks). Today he is not only coping but landed a job with a very desirable organization and received two desirable promotions in three years.

So if *you* are at the edge of hopelessness, by all means consider short-term therapy today. Don't wait until you step into the career world. Here's how to find a reliable therapist:

- Ask the Career Counseling Department or, more likely, the Psychology Department for referrals.

- Write to the International Association of Counseling Services, Inc. (Two Skyline Place, Suite 400, 5203 Leesburg Pike, Falls Church, VA 22041) for The Directory of Counseling Services, which lists accredited sources. (Cost is $6.00.)

- Consult the nearest office of the American Psychological Association.

- Ask your physician if he can offer suggestions or inquire for you.

Undoubtedly, this is one of the most nerve-wracking times of your life. So many students in the closing days of their college careers talk about "leaving the womb." That metaphor is entirely accurate.

Graduates and soon-to-be grads are about to take their first breath in a world entirely new to you—the world of careers. Like most newborns, you will enter kicking and screaming. The next chapter will give you a better idea of how to cope with the inevitable stresses and strains of "birth."

# 12

---

# LEARNING HOW TO HANDLE STRESS NOW... AND FOR THE FUTURE

---

My dear, if you would only recognize that life is hard, things would be so much easier for you.

—Justice Brandeis to his daughter.

The most prevalent symptom of the Student Shock Syndrome is the increased difficulty its victims have handling stress. When someone badly reeling from the Syndrome's effects first enters the work force, the stress added by the unfamiliar environment and its requirements could lead to overwhelming anxiety —unless one learns to control stress effectively.

And, of course, stress doesn't care if you've had one job or one hundred. Whatever your age or experience, stress is something you will have to handle, both at work and in your personal life.

# Stress—What It Is

The best first step to handling stress is understanding what it is.

There is no more reliable source on stress than Dr. Hans Selye He reminds us in his book, <u>Stress Without Distress</u> (The New American Library, Inc.), that although their stress-producing factors, which he calls *stressors,* are different, all people experience essentially the same biological stress response.

"Stress," says Selye, "is the nonspecific response of the body to any demand made upon it." He notes that while each demand placed on our bodies is unique (when exposed to cold we shiver to produce more heat, blood vessels in our skin contract to reduce loss of heat or, when exposed to heat, we sweat), "all agents to which we are exposed also produce a nonspecific increase in the need to perform adaptive functions and thereby to re-establish normalcy. This is independent of the specific activity that caused the rise in requirements."

Stress is not something to be avoided. The fact is, it *cannot* be avoided, notes Selye. When we say another person is "under stress," we actually mean excessive stress—*distress*..

There are all kinds of opportunities for keeping stress in its proper place, so that you can indeed make the most of your life. Remember these opportunities and the first 90 days on the job and beyond will go more smoothly.

Let's start with some of Dr. Selye's recommendations:

- Admit that there is no perfection, but in each category of achievement something is tops; be satisfied to strive for that!

- Whatever situation you meet in life, consider first whether it is really worth fighting for.

- Try to keep your mind constantly on the pleasant aspects of life and on actions which can improve your situation. Try to forget everything that is irrevocably ugly or painful. This is perhaps the most efficient way of minimizing stress.

- Even after the greatest defeats, take stock of all your achievements. Such conscious stock-taking is most effective in re-establishing the self-confidence necessary for future success.

- When faced with a task which is very painful yet indispensable to achieve your aim, don't procrastinate.

- Don't forget that there is no ready-made success formula that would suit everybody.

How prone are *you* to a great deal of stress—or distress? The following evaluation measures your current level of stress—your Personal Stress Index. The higher your PSI, the more attention stress deserves if you want to make the most of your life.

## The Barksdale Personal Stress Index

It is essential that you answer these statements according to how you actually feel or behave, rather than according to any concepts you have about how you "should" or "shouldn't" feel or behave. On a scale of 0 to 4, rate how strongly you identify with the following statements—0 being the least, 4 the most. The more strongly you identify with these statements, the higher your over-all score:

1. I am easily angered by others' undesirable attitudes and behavior.
2. I feel trapped by circumstances, demands and obligations.
3. I have a compulsive need to do "more" and "better."
4. I often put off doing things that I feel I ought to do now.

5. I experience insecurity and anxiety about my future.

6. I have an intense need for appreciation, love and caring.

7. I have a strong need for recognition and respect.

8. I have a compulsive need to meet others' requests.

9. I deeply resent unfair situations and events.

10. I do not get the recognition and credit I feel I deserve.

11. I have an intense need for attention and approval.

12. I find responsibility difficult to handle.

13. I have an intense need for the confirmation and agreement of others.

14. I find my life unfulfilled and meaningless.

15. I often feel inadequate, inferior, unworthy and guilty.

16. I am extremely impatient and easily frustrated.

17. I have a compulsive need to prove my worth.

18. I find it difficult to make decisions and stick to them.

19. I am harsh and demanding with myself.

20. I have a strong need to control people, situations and events.

21. I blame myself for mistakes, defeats and failures.

22. I experience anxiety about undertaking new endeavors.

23. I worry a great deal about my work and my loved ones.

24. I have a driving need to win—to be the "best."

25. I am very critical of people and displeasing be-
    havior.

To find your PSI, simply add up your scores on the 25
stress statements. Your PSI will fall somewhere between 0 and
100. A PSI of 5 or less indicates an exceptionally low level of
stress. A PSI of 20 or less indicates a favorable level. A PSI
between 20 and 50 indicates a definite handicap to one's well-
being. A PSI of more than 50 indicates a damaging level of stress
that, if prolonged indefinitely, could well be higher than the
human organism can tolerate.

Use the Barksdale Personal Stress Evaluation halfway
through your first 90 days on the job. It may help you to take
stock, develop a new sense of direction.

# How High Achievers
# Handle Stress

Why do some people never let stress get to them, no matter
how great the pressures they face? Here are some techniques
winners use for coping with stress:

- They recognize the need to determine whether
  given situations demand fight or flight. High
  achievers know that sometimes it's best to walk
  away from a stressful situation; other times
  demand a fight, come what may.

    Suggestion: Think back on recent stressors
    you faced and how you reacted. Doing so can be a
    valuable learning experience.

- They are not pessimistic. High achievers know
  there are stressors to face, that some of life's
  stresses can debilitate, or worse. They also know
  that nothing worthwhile was ever accomplished
  without a struggle.

- They have learned good health is essential for handling stress. As Peter J. Steincrohn, M.D., put it in his book, How To Master Your Fears, "We must accept the fact that the mind is not an extension of the body; that it does not exist apart from the rest of you. The mind is of body. As the body goes so does the mind, and vice versa."
- They know they hold their destiny in their own hands.
- They make physical activity a way of life. It is the most natural stress reducer.

Other tips for reducing stress:

- Know when and where tension is being stored in the body (tightening of muscles in the jaw, shoulders, neck, or back), stress that can develop into headaches, ulcers, or worse. (My consulting work includes acute care hospitals in the National Medical Enterprises, Inc. system and others. Doctors I know agree with medical authorities who say that 50 to 80 percent of diseases are stress-related.)
- Take notice of how your body is aligned during the day. If your career will require you to sit in the same position for hours at a time, learn the simple but critical stress-reducing ways of sitting properly—sitting with your back as straight as possible and with support for the lower back.
- Use stretching as a stress management technique. While most of us will stretch automatically when an area of our body is stiff and sore, we should actually stretch consciously and with awareness so as to establish more control for releasing tension.

    Perhaps you are already doing this in between long hours of study. This stretching can include tightening shoulder muscles more, for example, when you feel them tensing upward, then releasing them. You can do the same with arms or legs.

• Breathe properly and you can overcome anxiety, eliminate stress, and cut down on fatigue. This means you have to have Total Breath. You do this by starting to inhale slowly, beginning to breathe a few inches below your navel. Let your stomach expand as if it were a balloon being filled with air. Then, let your ribs expand—up and outward to the sides—and let your chest cavity expand to its fullest.

To complete the process, exhale in the same manner, forcing the air first out of the stomach area, then upwards to the chest. Exhalation is a way to release tension.

I can guarantee that this breathing process will help you before or after an exam, before or after a stressful situation in your career—a job interview, your performance review, or the big day when you make your first presentation to a group of superiors.

• Mix positivism with some negativism. Don't believe the euphoric positivists who say, "You can be anything you want to be." Instead, make sure your goals are realistic and attainable.

Dr. Robert Eliot, renowned stress authority who wrote <u>Is It Worth Dying For?</u> (Bantam), urges us to lower our expectations and raise our possibility of success: "The impossible dream makes great theater, but in real life it often sets up a formula for stress and depression."

So *accept* stress, study how it relates to your very special circumstance, and learn the effective options you have for staying in control.

I hope this book will be helpful to everyone going through the difficult transition of college life to career life, or from one job to another. As I've tried to convince you, the best way to handle the transition is to plan for it, to make sure that it is right for you in as many ways as possible.

Is it the right career? Is it the right job in that career? Is it the right company offering the job? Is it the right boss at that company? These questions must be answered *before* you accept the job, one hopes, not after you've already gotten started on 90 days of Hell!

To answer those questions, however, requires preparation. To know what career is best for you, you must get to know yourself a little better, to be familiar and comfortable with your strengths and weaknesses.

Then, once you make the difficult move to a new job, follow the advice of sports coaches everywhere: "Play within yourself." If you do that—to the best of your abilities—you will be successful and happy.

What more could you want?

# Index

# WHERE TO FIND
# WHAT *YOU* NEED
# TO SURVIVE

- **Your First Resume: The Essential Comprehensive Guide for Anyone Entering or Reentering the Job Market (2nd Edition)** by Ronald W. Fry. Paper, 8 1/2 x 11, 192 pp., $10.95

- **Work in the New Economy: Careers and Job Seeking into the 21st Century,** by Robert Wegmann, Robert Chapman and Miriam Johnson, Paper, 6 x 9, 303 pp., $14.95.

- **The Complete Guide to International Jobs & Careers** by Drs. Ron & Caryl Krannich, Paper, 6 x 9, 236 pp., $13.95

- **Your First Book of Wealth** by A. David Silver ISBN 0-934829-47-0, Paper, 6 x 9, 224 pp., $10.95.

- **High Impact Resumes and Letters,** 4th Edition, by Krannich and Banis, Paper, 7 x 10, 180 pp., $12.95

- **Interview for Success,** by Drs. Caryl & Ron Krannich. Paper, 6 x 9, 176 pp., $11.95

- **The Complete Guide to Public Employment,** by Drs. Ron and Caryl Krannich, Paper, 6 x 9, 483 pp., $15.95.

- **Careering & Recareering for the 1990s** by Ronald L. Krannich Paper, 6 x 9, 192 pp., $12.95

- **Network Your Way to Job and Career Success** by Drs. Ron & Caryl Krannich, Paper, 6 x 9, 180 pp., $11.95

## TO ORDER ANY TITLES OR REQUEST A CATALOG:

### CALL 1-800-CAREER-1
### TO USE YOUR MASTERCARD OR VISA.

**Or send price as indicated, plus appropriate shipping and handling (please enclose $2.50 per order and $1.00 per title for each book ordered) to:**

The Career Press
62 Beverly Rd., PO Box 34
Hawthorne, NJ 07507